Drink to Your Good Health With Smoothies Like:

- *Immune Booster.* Carrot, fresh pineapple, and chunk ginger juiced with mashed sweet potato, raw cashews, and ice. The perfect antidote for anyone who's "under the weather."
- *Arabian Nights and Sweet Dreams.* Take soy milk, sesame butter (tahini), and grated citrus peel. Add banana and fresh orange. Flavor with vanilla and enrich with lecithin. You'll have an exotic, mineral-rich smoothie.
- *Wild Berry Bright Eyes.* Mix blueberries, blackberries, and raspberry extract with Wild Berry Zinger ice cubes, then blend in soy milk and honey. It's a creamy, colorful smoothie that's great for your eyes—and your taste buds.
- *Carbo Power Pack.* Pour tangy apple juice into a blender along with yogurt, fresh blueberries, frozen peaches, and other ingredients. Flavor with almond and vanilla extracts. Ideal energy on any sports day.
- *Orange Coconut Creamsicle-in-a-Glass.* Cut oranges into chunks. Add milk of choice, grated coconut, vanilla, honey, and ice. Here's a calcium-rich drink that's yummy—and the kids will love it!
- *Berry Smoothie.* Combine one sweet apple, cranberries, and creamy low-fat yogurt. Garnish with a sprig of mint or strawberry for a treat that's also food for your bones.

OTHER BOOKS BY CHERIE CALBOM

The Juice Lady's Guide to Health

The Juice Lady's Juicing for High-Level Wellness
and Vibrant Good Looks

Knock Out the Fat Barbecue & Grilling Cookbook

The Healthy Gourmet

Juicing for Life

The Ultimate Smoothie BOOK

101 Delicious Recipes for Blender Drinks,
Frozen Desserts, Shakes and More!

CHERIE CALBOM

WARNER BOOKS
A Time Warner Company

Warner Books, Inc., 1271 Avenue of the Americas, New York, NY 10020
Visit our Web site at www.twbookmark.com
For information on Time Warner Trade Publishing's online publishing program, visit www.ipublish.com.

A Time Warner Company

Printed in the United States of America
First Printing: August 2001
10 9 8 7 6 5 4 3 2 1

Library of Congress Cataloging-in-Publication Data

Calbom, Cherie.
The ultimate smoothie book : 101 delicious recipes for blender drinks, frozen desserts, shakes, and more! / Cherie Calbom.
p. cm.
Includes index.
ISBN 0-446-67775-2
1. Blenders (Cookery) 2. Smoothies (Beverages) I. Title.

TX840.B5 C35 2001
641.5'89—dc21

Text design by Meryl Sussman Levavi/Digitext
Cover design by Diane Luger
Cover photography by Nancy Palubniak

Contents

Recipes 67

Acknowledgments

I wish to express my deep and lasting appreciation to the people who have assisted me with this book, especially Vicki Chelf, friend and co-author of my book *Cooking for Life,* who joined me in Colorado, lending her exceptional culinary skills and delightful approach to recipe creation in helping me invent over 100 fabulous recipes. Vicki, you're the best!

A sincere thank-you to Steven Sapienza, R.D., of Nutritional Analysis Consultants, for his expert nutritional analyses and quick response to my requests. You've been such a delight to work with through the years.

A very special thanks to Wendy Keller, my creative

agent, for her help and guidance, and suggestions through the years. I'm so glad I found you.

Many thanks to my editors, Diana Baroni and Molly Chehak, for their input in making this book a success.

Finally, my deep gratitude and continued appreciation to John, my husband, who has been my official taste tester for more smoothies than any human being may ever have been asked to drink in a short period of time. Thank you most of all for being my strength and cheering me on to new successes each year.

Introduction

I've devoted my life to teaching people how to improve and maintain their health through better food choices. I'm committed to this goal because I turned my own health around—from suffering chronic fatigue syndrome and fibromyalgia in my late twenties to enjoying vibrant health today. I'm thrilled to have this opportunity to create a smoothies recipe book that can give you up-to-date information on choosing the best ingredients to make the most delicious and the healthiest smoothies possible. What could be any better for you than fresh fruit, soy milk or yogurt, and ice! Yet one of the reasons smoothies are so popular is that they taste decadent—like an ice-cream milk shake—but offer a terrific alternative that's low in fat and high in nutrition.

Talk about popular! *Entrepreneur* magazine has rated the smoothie industry as the hottest business idea in 1998 and 1999. "Smoothie bars" are sprouting up in New York, Chicago, and Los Angeles. If these major cities are taking the lead, it won't be long before Little League teams in Syracuse, Springfield, and Santa Rosa are hanging out in the "bar" after the game, sipping on rejuvenating vitamins bundled in a freshly made smoothie.

Smoothies are an especially smart choice for kids. Typically, the diet of American children consists of bread, beef, cheese, French fries, chips, cakes, cookies, candy, ice cream, and sodas. (Read the book *Carbohydrate Addicted Kids* by Drs. Rachel F. and Richard F. Heller.) This kind of unbalanced diet wreaks havoc on a child's nervous and hormonal systems. Sodas, for example, are made up of phosphoric acid, caffeine, sugar (typically 11 teaspoons in one 12-ounce can) or aspartame, caramel coloring, carbon dioxide, and aluminum (leached from cans). Phosphoric acid in sodas can cause an imbalance between calcium and phosphorus in the body, causing a person to be fidgety, nervous, and hyper. No wonder ADD (attention deficit disorder) and ADHD (attention deficit hyperactivity disorder) are on the rise and prescriptions for Ritalin have increased by 600 percent in the last ten years. Kids need a lot more fresh vegetables and fruits in their diet to maintain health than they are typically getting. That can be a challenge for many parents. But almost all kids like shakes and smoothies, which can replace sodas, and you can take vegetables and fruits they normally wouldn't eat, and blend them up in seconds.

Indeed, smoothies make good sense for the whole family. Statistics show that on an average day 41 percent of us eat no fruit at all, 72 percent eat no vitamin C–rich fruit, 82 percent eat no cruciferous vegetables (broccoli, cauliflower, cabbage), and 84 percent eat no high-fiber foods. More than 70 percent of the food we eat has been processed and mostly stripped of health-giving fiber, natural oils, vitamins, minerals, enzymes, and phytonutrients. Depleted soils, lengthy storage, and poor food handling also contribute to the depletion of nutrients.

That's where smoothies can help you and your family fill in the gaps. Vitamin C is possibly one of the body's most important antioxidants. It has been shown to lower blood pressure, prevent kidney disease, reduce the risk of cancer, boost the immune system to prevent viral infections, and strengthen blood vessels to prevent easy bruising and gum diseases. You can easily add vitamin C–rich fruits and vegetables like strawberries, papaya, oranges, parsley, and spinach to smoothies and reap the benefits. You can fortify your bones with calcium, magnesium, vitamin K, and boron by adding dark greens to smoothies along with soy milk or silken tofu, seeds, nuts, or dried fruit. And you can get the amazing cancer-preventive, immune-enhancing benefits of beta-carotene and other carotenes by blending up orange, red, and dark green fruits and vegetables.

Smoothies make such good sense for people on the go because they can be made in minutes. You can drink your vitamins on the run! In the pages that follow, I have created recipes for kids, workouts, weight loss, healthy pregnancy, new parents, coffee-break energizers, health-and-healing combinations, and much, much more. My "nutrisips" will help you know just what's in the smoothie recipe you're blending that makes it nutritionally special. Then, as you sip your yummy, somewhat decadent drink, you'll know you're doing something really good for your body, not just your taste buds. Enjoy! . . . To health!

The Ultimate Smoothie BOOK

Getting Started

Making Fresh Juice

I use a lot of fresh juices in my smoothie recipes. You may think that's just because I'm the Juice Lady, but my love of fresh vegetable and fruit juices goes back many years before the Juice Lady was born. I turned my health around from continual illness and fatigue to the vibrant health I enjoy today because I changed my diet and started drinking an abundance of fresh vegetable juices along with a little fruit juice. Though all of the recipes in this book can be made in a blender, I recommend using a juicer as well. If you don't own a juicer, I highly recommend that you invest in one. You'll be investing in your health and that of the people you love.

Choosing the Right Juicer

To get the most from juicing, it's very important that you get the right juicer; it can make the difference between juicing nearly every day and not juicing at all. It's important to distinguish between a blender and a juicer. You will use a blender for making smoothies. It liquefies or purees everything placed in it and does not separate pulp from juice. A juice machine, on the other hand, separates liquid from pulp. If you think you really don't need a juicer and that it might be a good idea to have carrot, celery, or beet pulp in your juice for extra fiber (some manufacturers tell you you should), I can tell you from experience that those residues taste like juicy sawdust. For the best texture and flavor, I recommend you use a juicer. Look for these features:

- Choose a machine with adequate horsepower (hp). I recommend one with 0.5 hp. Weak machines with low horsepower ratings must run at extremely high revolutions per minute (rpm). A machine's rpm does not accurately reflect its ability to perform effectively because rpm is calculated when the juicer is running idle, not while it is juicing. When you feed produce into a low-power machine, the rpm will be reduced dramatically, sometimes stopping the juicer completely. I've "killed" a few juicers on the first carrot.

- Look for a machine that has electronic circuitry that sustains blade speed during juicing.
- Make sure the machine can juice tough, hard vegetables and fruits, such as pineapple skins, watermelon rinds, carrots, and beets, along with leafy greens such as parsley, lettuce, spinach, and herbs. Make sure it doesn't need a special citrus attachment.
- Look for a large feed tube so that you don't have to cut your produce into little pieces.
- A juicer that ejects pulp is best; it allows for continuous, nonstop juicing. Juicers that keep the pulp inside the machine require that it constantly be scooped out. Many of them have to be washed out before you can continue juicing.
- Choose a juicer that has only a few parts to clean and make sure you can clean them easily. The more parts a juicer has, and the more complicated the parts to wash, the longer it will take you to clean up and put the juicer back together. That makes it likely you won't use your machine very much. Also, choose a juicer that has a juice bowl that won't stain. Light plastic stains easily and it is hard to get the stains out.

My top recommendation for a juicer is my own Juice Lady juice machine available from Salton. It has all these features, including a stainless-steel juice bowl.

Tips for Juicing

1. Wash all produce before juicing; fruit and vegetable washes are available from many grocers and health food stores. Cut away all moldy, bruised, or damaged areas before juicing.
2. Use organic or unsprayed (transitional) produce whenever possible to ensure that you have the purest juices. (See page 8 for more information on organically grown produce.)
3. Because the skins of oranges, tangerines, and grapefruits contain indigestible, volatile oils that can cause digestive problems and taste bitter, always peel these citrus fruits before juicing. (Lemon and lime peels can be juiced if organic.) You should leave as much of the white pithy part on the citrus fruit as possible, since it contains the most vitamin C and bioflavonoids (phytonutrients with antioxidant activity). Always peel mangoes and papayas, since their skins contain an irritant that is harmful when eaten in quantity. Also, I recommend that you peel all produce that is not labeled organic, even though the largest concentration of nutrients is in and next to the skin; the peels and skins of sprayed fruits and vegetables have the largest concentration of pesticides.
4. Remove pits, stones, and hard seeds from fruits such as peaches, plums, apricots, cherries, and mangoes. Softer seeds from oranges, lemons, watermelon, cantaloupe, grapes, and apples can be juiced without a problem.

Because of their trace-element composition, large quantities of apple seeds should not be juiced for young children; they should be okay for most adults.

5. The stems and leaves of most produce, such as beet stems and leaves, strawberry caps, and small grape stems can be included in the juicing process; they offer nutrients as well. Larger grape stems should be discarded, as they can dull the juicer blade. Carrot and rhubarb greens should be removed because they contain toxic substances.
6. Most fruits and vegetables have a high water content, which makes them ideal for juicing. Those with much less water, such as bananas, mangoes, papayas, and avocados, will not juice well. They can be used in smoothies and cold soups by combining them in a blender with fresh juice or milk of choice.
7. Most fruits and vegetables should be cut into sections or strips that will fit your juicer's feed tube.
8. Juice can be stored in an airtight, opaque container in the refrigerator or a thermos for up to twenty-four hours; light, heat, and air will destroy nutrients quickly. Melon and cabbage juices do not store well. Be aware that the longer juice sits before you drink it, the more nutrients it loses. If juice turns brown, it has oxidized and lost a large amount of its food value. After twenty-four to forty-eight hours, it may become spoiled.
9. Place a plastic bag—the kind that you find free in the produce section of a grocery store—in the pulp receptacle of your juicer. When you are done juicing, you can toss the pulp or use it in cooking or composting, but you won't need to wash the receptacle.

Organically Grown Ingredients

Organic foods are those grown without pesticides or chemical fertilizers. Nonorganic foods, often referred to as "commercial," are grown with a variety of toxic chemicals, many of which are known to be or suspected of being carcinogenic and which damage the environment.

Choosing organically grown produce whenever possible is good for the taste buds. Many famous chefs across America think so and are opting for organic food when it is available. But the primary reason for choosing organic foods, even when they cost a few pennies more, is for their health benefits. First, and foremost, pesticides are not good for anyone's body—they can pose long-term health risks like cancer and birth defects as well as immediate health concerns such as acute intoxication, with symptoms that include vomiting, diarrhea, blurred vision, tremors, convulsions, and nerve damage.

But is organically grown food more nutritious? That is the question that's been posed by critics for years. Intrigued by the claims that organics are better, researchers at Rutgers University decided to look for some answers. They compared the mineral content of commercially grown produce with that of organically grown. The results were astounding! Commercially grown spinach had only 3 percent as much iron as organically grown spinach and less than 1 percent of the manganese. Commercial cabbage had 70 percent less calcium than its organic counterpart. Organically grown lettuce had 70 percent more potassium than commercial lettuce. Tomatoes grown commercially had only 8 percent as much magnesium as the organic tomatoes, and snap beans had only 3 percent as much manganese as the organic beans.

Organic produce is richer in nutrients as a result of the practice of composting and crop rotation utilized by most organic farmers. Composting is necessary when chemical fertilizers are not used, and composts replenish the soil with minerals. For your health's sake, I encourage you to choose organically grown produce whenever possible. When it is not available, ask your grocer to carry it for you. The more requests made for organically grown food, the more available it will be, and the less it will cost.

When choosing organically grown food, look for labels marked "certified organic." Such labels mean that the produce has been cultivated according to uniform standards that are verified by independent state or private organizations. Certification includes inspection of farms and processing facilities, record keeping, and testing of soil and water for pesticides—all to ensure that growers have met government standards.

If you see a label that says "transitional" or "transitional organic," this means the food was grown on a farm that recently converted, or is in the process of converting, from chemical to organic farming.

In addition, avoid bioengineered foods. A recent landmark lawsuit against the FDA revealed internal reports showing such foods not to be completely safe. Foods produced through recombinant DNA technology entail a unique set of risks over that of their conventionally produced counterparts, such as toxins and allergens.

Also, avoid irradiated food. Producers use gamma-ray radiation to kill pests and germs in stored food, and to increase the food's shelf life. But eating irradiated food is not something that can promote health. The average doses of radiation used to decontaminate most foods can be up to 5 million times that of a typical chest x-ray. This practice destroys vitamins and minerals. It also generates harmful byproducts such as free radicals, toxins that can damage cells, and harmful chemicals known as radiolytic products that include formaldehyde and benzene.

Fruits and Vegetables

Apple There are many varieties of apples, the most popular being Red and Golden Delicious; other well-known varieties include Winesap, McIntosh, Jonathan, Rome, Gravenstein, Stayman, Cortland, Granny Smith, and Newton Pippins.

Season: Apples are available all year long, since there are summer, fall, and winter varieties. In the spring they have probably been pulled from cold storage. Choose firm, crisp apples without soft spots, bruises, or wrinkles. Apples picked at maturity will have high color and will have the best flavor and texture.

Preparation: Simply wash an apple if it's organic. Peel it if it's not organic or if it is waxed; although the peel is rich in nutrients, remove it to eliminate waxes and pesticides. If juicing the apple, cut it into wedges that fit your juice extractor feed tube; you can juice the core. Seeds should not hurt an adult; avoid seeds for children under two. To freeze, remove the core, cut the apple into one-inch chunks, and place them in a freezer bag.

Nutritional content: Apples are a fairly good source of chromium and manganese and an excellent source of pectins—soluble fiber that helps regulate blood sugar levels and cholesterol. They are low in fruit sugars, making them a good fruit choice for people sensitive to sugars, such as diabetics. Pectin also promotes good intestinal flora that help keep the colon healthy; it also acts as a natural laxative. Additionally, apples contain polyphenols, phytochemicals that have antiviral and antibacterial functions, glutathione, a powerful antioxidant, and malic acid, a binder of heavy metals. No wonder we've been told that an apple a day keeps the doctor away!

APRICOT About five varieties are commercially available, including the Blenheim, Tilton, Early Montgamet, and Wenatchee.

Season: Apricots are available May through August, but their peak is June and July. Choose plump, juicy-looking apricots with a uniform golden-orange color. Ripe apricots will yield to gentle pressure when touched. Avoid soft, mushy, or hard apricots and pale yellow or greenish fruit—a sign they are underripe.

Preparation: Wash apricots and cut them in half; remove the stone. To freeze, cut them in one-inch chunks and place them in a freezer bag.

Nutritional content: Apricots are rich in carotenes and flavonoids. Beta-carotene is a powerful antioxidant and is also converted by the body to vitamin A as it is needed. Flavonoids work with vitamin C, making it much more effective in its functions. Dried apricots are very rich in beta-carotene and a good source of calcium. To use dried apricots in a smoothie, soak in a little water from one hour to overnight (just barely cover to preserve flavor; add the water to the smoothie).

AVOCADO California varieties, known as Haas, are small, have a rough skin, and range in color from dark green to black; Florida varieties are much larger, with a smooth, bright green skin.

Season: California avocados are available year-round; Florida avocados are available August to January with a peak in October and November. For immediate use, choose avocados that yield to gentle pressure. For use in a few days, buy firm fruit and let it ripen at room temperature; or to speed ripening, place in a room-temperature, dark spot like a paper sack or drawer. Avoid avocados with dark or soft spots or a cracked surface, indicative of decay. An avocado is no longer good when it is soft or the pit rattles when you shake it.

Preparation: Cut in half, remove skin and seed, and cut into chunks. Avocados do not freeze well.

Nutritional content: Avocados are a good source of vitamin B6, folic acid, iron, magnesium, phosphorus, potassium, and protein, and an excellent source of oleic acid and glutathione. Oleic acid is an essential fatty acid that is a heart-healthy fat; it's also cancer preventative and good for your skin and hair. Avocados are rich in the enzyme glutathione, an antioxidant that defends the body from free-radical attack. Also, a small California avocado (about 4 ounces) yields around 700 milligrams of potassium, an electrolyte that is associated with healthy blood pressure.

Banana Bananas come primarily from Costa Rica, Honduras, and Panama.

Season: Bananas are available year-round. Look for bananas free of bruises, with the skin intact at both ends. Bananas that are slightly green indicate they have not been gassed to ripen them quickly.

Preparation: Peel bananas and cut into chunks. Bananas freeze well; you can place banana chunks in a freezer bag (always peel first) and store until ready to use—up to three or four weeks.

Nutritional content: An excellent source of potassium, the banana is also a good source of vitamin B6, magnesium, iron, and chromium. Potassium is an electrolyte that is lost with the use of prescription diuretics and strenuous exercise. High intake of potassium is associated with lowered risk of hypertension.

BELL PEPPER In America, the leading varieties of bell peppers include Bellringer, Bell Boy, California Wonder, Merrimack Wonder, and Worldbeater.

Season: Bell peppers are available all year long, with peak season June through September. Choose firm, shiny bell peppers that are heavy for their size and preferably unwaxed. The skin should be smooth, without soft spots, and the color dark, whether green, red, or yellow.

Preparation: Wash bell peppers, cut in half, and remove the seeds and stem. Cut into chunks. Freezing is not recommended.

Nutritional content: Bell peppers are rich in beta-carotene and vitamin C, powerful antioxidants that are immune-building and help fight infections and disease.

BLACKBERRY Several varieties of blackberries have been grown in the United States since the 1800s, including a thornless variety. Leading producers in the U.S. are Texas and Oregon.

Season: Blackberries are available from May through August. Choose blackberries that are brightly colored; avoid berries that are partly green or off-color. Look for berries that are fresh, solid, and dry; check the bottom of the carton for wet or moldy berries.

Preparation: Just before using blackberries, place them in a bowl of cool water and stir them gently with your hand or a wooden spoon. Drain the water and repeat; drain in a colander. Remove all stems and pick out any damaged or moldy berries. Blackberries freeze well; when they are dry, place them in a freezer bag and store in the freezer until ready to use. They can be stored three to four weeks.

Nutritional content: Blackberries are a good source of folic acid, magnesium, potassium, and iron, and rich in flavonoids, especially anthocyanidins and proanthocyanidins. These phytonutrients are especially helpful in strengthening collagen structure; collagen is the major protein structure of the bones, adds elasticity to the skin, and is also protective against coronary disease.

BLUEBERRY Blueberries have been cultivated since the early 1900s, but the wild variety, while smaller than the commercial types, is still superior in taste. The favorite cultivated types are high-bush and low-bush blueberries. States leading in production are Maine, Michigan,

New Jersey, North Carolina, Oregon, and Washington.

Season: Blueberries are available between May and September. Choose clean, plump, well-rounded blueberries that are fairly uniform in size. Look for bright, deep blue, black, or purple berries that appear slightly frosted. The best berries are fresh, firm, and dry. Check the bottom of the container for wet or moldy berries.

Preparation: To wash, place berries in a bowl of cool water and stir them gently with your hand or a wooden spoon. Drain the water and repeat; drain in a colander. Pick off the stems and remove any damaged or moldy berries. Blueberries freeze well; when they are dry, put them in a freezer bag and store in the freezer until ready to use. Freeze no more than three to four weeks.

Nutritional content: Blueberries have some chromium and are a good source of flavonoids, especially anthocyanidins and proanthocyanidins. Just like the cranberry, blueberries contain a compound that prevents adherence of bacteria to the bladder wall, thus making the little blueberry a mighty bladder-infection fighter, too. During World War II, British Royal Air Force pilots consumed bilberry (a close relative of blueberry) preserves to improve their night vision. After the war, studies confirmed that the berries do indeed improve nighttime vision and lead to quicker adjustment to darkness.

CARROT Carrots are categorized according to color and size: red, yellow-orange, or white, and short, medium, or long. Carrots are an easy crop and are grown in nearly every state.

Season: Carrots are available all year. Choose large, firm, smooth, well-shaped carrots with good orange color. Avoid rough, cracked, or pale carrots. A green tinge at the top of a carrot indicates it was sunburned and could have a bitter taste. A mass of leafy stems indicates a large, woody core. Avoid flabby or shriveled carrots and trimmed carrots that are sprouting.

Preparation: Simply scrub an organic carrot with a vegetable brush; peel the carrot if it's not organic. Always cut off the green tops; they contain toxic substances and are inedible. If juicing the carrots, cut them to fit the juice machine feed tube. Freezing carrots for smoothies is not recommended. However, you can freeze carrot juice in a covered container.

Nutritional content: Carrots are a very rich source of beta-carotene and also provide vitamin E, calcium, magnesium, phosphorus, sodium, potassium, iron, copper, manganese, zinc, chromium, and vanadium. Carrot juice has been used to ease menopausal symptoms and to contribute to the prevention of cancer, especially breast cancer.

CHERRY There are more than a thousand varieties of

cherries, but Bing is the most popular. Cherries are grown in every state, with Washington, Oregon, California, and Idaho being the major growers of sweet cherries.

Season: Sweet cherries are available from April through August. Choose dark-colored cherries that are shiny and full; they are the sweetest. They should be firm to the touch, but not hard. Avoid cherries with dark-colored stems.

Preparation: Discard mushy or moldy cherries. Then rinse the cherries under cold running water, and dry them in a colander. Cut them in half and remove the pits and stems.

Nutritional content: Cherries are a good source of potassium and flavonoids, especially anthocyanidins and proanthocyanidins. These plant pigments work with vitamin C to strengthen collagen, a fibrous protein in connective tissue. This makes cherries and dark-colored berries good for athletes, who put a lot of stress and strain on joints. Cherries have also been used as a traditional treatment for gout.

Coconut Some coconuts are grown in Florida and sold to tourists. Coconuts sold in markets are typically imported from Honduras, Panama, and the Dominican Republic.

Season: Coconuts can be found year-round in markets, but peak months are October, November, and December. Choose a coconut that seems heavy for its size. Shake it; a good coconut will have liquid sloshing around inside. Bypass coconuts without liquid; this indicates the fruit has spoiled. Also, avoid coconuts with wet or moldy "eyes"—the three dark soft spots at the top of the shell.

Preparation: For starters, pierce the softest eye on a coconut shell with a knife or ice pick. Place the pierced part over a glass or bowl and let the liquid drain out. To crack a coconut shell, place the drained coconut in a 375° F. oven for five to ten minutes, then remove it and tap it forcefully with a hammer. The coconut will break apart easily, and the flesh will loosen a bit from the shell. Break it into pieces for smoothies. Keep unused coconut meat refrigerated in a plastic bag.

Nutritional content: Coconut is rich in magnesium, manganese, and copper. Manganese is an important mineral in immune support and glucose tolerance. Manganese requirements are greatly increased during pregnancy and the rapid growth of childhood.

CRANBERRY Most commercial cranberries are grown in the northeast, especially Massachusetts. Wisconsin, New Jersey, Washington, and Oregon are also major producers.

Season: Cranberries can be found in most markets

from September through March, although peak season is October through December. Choose firm, round, plump cranberries that are brightly colored and lustrous. Avoid shriveled, dull, soft, or yellowed berries.

Preparation: Pick through the cranberries and discard all bad ones. Rinse the remaining cranberries under cold running water and dry them in a colander. Cranberries freeze well. Dry them before placing in a freezer bag and storing in the freezer. They will usually last several months when frozen. It is a good idea to buy them in season and freeze for future needs, since they are to be found in markets only a few months out of the year.

Nutritional content: Cranberries have been shown in scientific studies to be quite effective in treating bladder infections. They contain a substance known as "cranberry factor" that keeps bacteria from adhering to the bladder wall. Cranberries also contain the flavonoids, anthocyanidins, and proanthocyanidins.

CUCUMBER In the United States, Florida supplies about one-third of the cucumbers; other major producers are California, North and South Carolina, New York, and New Jersey.

Season: Cucumbers are available throughout the year, with peak season from May through August. Choose firm, bright, well-shaped cucumbers that are medium to dark green and 5 to 7 inches in length. Bypass old cucumbers that appear dull or yellowish and cucumbers that are too large. Also, avoid cucumbers that are puffy, withered, or shriveled; they can be rubbery or bitter tasting.

Preparation: Peel cucumbers that are nonorganic (pesticide sprayed) or waxed. Organic cucumbers just need to be rinsed; however, for freezing, peel cucumbers, cut them in half, and chop into one-inch chunks. Place the chunks in a freezer bag and store in the freezer until ready to use. Cucumbers should last in the freezer three to four weeks.

Nutritional content: Cucumbers are best known for their water content. The skin is a good source of the mineral silica, which contributes to the strength of connective tissue—muscles, tendons, ligaments, bone, and cartilage. Silica is also known for its ability to improve the complexion and increase the health of the skin.

DATE The most popular varieties of dates include Deglect Noor, Khadrawi, Thoory, or "bread," Halawi, and Medjool. Dates can be found in most markets and natural food stores.

Season: Dates are available in the market all year long. Choose plump, smooth, chocolate-colored dates that have a bit of shine. Avoid dates that are dark, dry, crusty, and cracked. Blackening of the flesh causes a bitter taste. Domestic dates are often pasteurized to prevent mold. Avoid dates packed with corn syrup or sugar; they are sweet enough as they are. Also, bypass dates treated with the preservatives sulfur dioxide and sorbic acid, potassium sorbate, and sodium benzoate. Soft and semisoft dates keep best in the refrigerator; they can also be frozen.

Preparation: Cut out the pits and chop the dates into small pieces. Date puree is easiest to use. To make, combine pitted dates in a blender with just enough water to cover and blend until mixture is smooth.

Nutritional content: Dates are quite rich in potassium, an electrolyte that is essential for maintaining fluid balance; they are also a good source of calcium, magnesium, and phosphorus—needed for strong bones and teeth—and iron for energy.

FENNEL This vegetable can be found in most supermarkets and many natural food markets. It is also commonly grown in home vegetable and herb gardens.

Season: Sweet fennel is available summer, fall, and winter; peak season is October through January.

Preparation: Simply rinse the fennel; leaves can be used as an herb, as desired, or juiced. If juicing fennel, cut the bulb into chunks that will fit your juicer's feed tube. Freezing is not recommended.

Nutritional content: Fennel is most known for its medicinal effects. It has been noted for use as an intestinal antispasmodic; a carminative, a compound that relieves or expels gas; a stomachic, to tone and strengthen the stomach; and an anodyne, to relieve and soothe pain. Fennel also contains phytoestrogens, making it especially good for menopausal symptoms. It has also been used to help increase the flow of breast milk during lactation.

FIG The most popular varieties of dried figs are Calimyrna (tan color) and Mission (purplish black), less likely to be treated with sulfur. Calamata string figs, imported from Greece, are also unsulfured.

Season: Fresh figs are available June through September, with peak season in July and August. Look for figs that are fairly soft but not mushy. Avoid figs with breaks in the skin, which can cause rapid deterioration. Dried figs are available year-round.

Preparation: Simply wash fresh figs; remove the end stem. Fresh figs don't freeze well or last very long. Dried figs can be cut into small chunks for the blender or made into a puree (easiest to blend) by combining them with a little water in the blender and processing on high speed. Dried figs freeze well.

Nutritional content: Figs are rich in calcium, magnesium, potassium, and iron. Rich in minerals, figs make a good addition for a workout smoothie or an energizing drink.

GINGERROOT Gingerroot is grown in many areas of the world with warm climates. Almost all the gingerroot in the United States comes from Hawaii.

Season: Gingerroot is available in markets year-round. Choose ginger that is firm, plump, and heavy. Ginger that is not fresh is lightweight and wrinkled in appearance. Bypass roots with moldy or discolored ends. Small knobs growing on the main root indicate new growth and are usable.

Preparation: Just scrub organically grown gingerroot; peel nonorganic ginger. Cut off any damaged portions. For smoothies, you can juice ginger or grate it finely. Freezing is not recommended.

Nutritional content: One of the best sources of zinc—a powerful immune builder—ginger is also used for its medicinal qualities. It has been shown to lower cholesterol; it has anti-inflammatory properties; and it is used for migraine headaches. Known for its antinausea effects, it has long been used by pregnant women for morning sickness and by travelers for motion sickness.

GRAPEFRUIT Grapefruit comes in three colors: white, pink, and red (Ruby Red and Star Ruby), with pink and red being the sweetest. The United States produces the majority of the world's grapefruit, with Florida and Texas being the top producers, followed by California and Arizona.

Season: Grapefruit is available all year long, with October through April being peak season. Choose heavy, firm, well-rounded grapefruits with thin, smooth skins for the most juice and best flavor.

Preparation: Peel the outer skin whether juicing or adding grapefruit to your blender. The white part just below the skin is the part that is richest in nutrients, and I recommend that you use as much of that part of the grapefruit as possible. It will cause your smoothie to be just a slight bit more bitter tasting, however.

Nutritional content: Grapefruit is rich in flavonoids, vitamin C, pectin, potassium, and inositol, a member of the vitamin B complex. Grapefruit is good for the heart—it has been shown to normalize hematocrit levels; pectin lowers cholesterol; and potassium lowers blood pressure. It is also rich in cancer-preventative flavonoids—terpenes, limonenes, and coumarins.

GRAPE AND RAISIN Divided into four classes: wine, table, raisin, and sweet juice, grapes in the United States are varieties or hybrids of European stock. They include the blackish purple Concords and Ribiers, red Tokays and Emperors, and yellowish green Thompson seedless. California is the leading U.S. grape producer, followed by New York, Michigan, and Washington. There are several popular varieties of raisins, including the seedless Thompson, sultanas, muscats, and monukkas.

Season: Domestic grapes can be found from late June through March, and peak season is September through November. Look for grapes that are bright in color, plump, and firm. Choose deep-colored red or purple grapes and green grapes that have turned slightly yellow. Look for stems that are green and firm. Avoid grapes that are dry or brown- or black-speckled. Grapes are the most commonly sprayed crops, and their skins are thin; therefore they absorb chemicals easily. It is especially advantageous to purchase organically grown grapes. Organic raisins are about as rare as organic grapes but are worth the search since raisins are dried grapes. As with prunes, sorbate preservatives are often added to raisins because their sugars tend to rise to the surface, appearing as white crystals.

Preparation: For the blender, pick through any bad grapes and pick from the stems; rinse under cold running water. For juicing, you can leave small stems on grapes. Remove all thick stems so as not to dull your juicer blade. Grapes freeze well. For freezing, let them dry in a colander, place them in a freezer bag, and store in the freezer until ready to use. They can be stored for three to four weeks. Simply add raisins to the blender for smoothies; they can also be frozen.

Nutritional content: When you juice or blend grapes with seeds, you release the nutritional benefits of grape seed extract, which contains flavonoids used widely in Europe to treat varicose veins and other venous disorders. Grapes also contain a phytochemical known as resveratrol, the chemical responsible for the heart-+-healthy effects of red wine. Resveratrol also has demonstrated anti-cancer properties. Raisins are rich in inositol, one of the B-complex vitamins, calcium, magnesium, phosphorus, potassium, iron, and manganese.

KALE The most popular varieties are spring kale, with smooth leaves, and Scotch kale and Siberian blue kale, which have curly leaves. In the United States the major kale producers are Virginia, Maryland, New York, and New Jersey.

Season: Kale is available in markets all year long, with peak season being December through April. Look for kale that is crisp, firm, and deep green, with uniform color.

Preparation: Simply wash kale leaves. For juicing, bunch it up and push through your juicer's feed tube.

If adding directly to a blender, chop it into small pieces. Kale can be frozen.

Nutritional content: Rich in beta-carotene, kale has earned its reputation as the King of Calcium for good reason—it's one of the best sources of calcium found in nature; ounce for ounce it has more than double that of milk. It's a fabulous bone builder because it also contains vitamin K (a deficiency can lead to osteoporosis) and boron, which works much like estrogen to help prevent loss of calcium from bones.

Kiwifruit In the United States, California is the major producer of kiwifruit.

Season: Kiwifruit are usually available all year long in markets, but peak season is June through October. Choose kiwis that are firm but give slightly to pressure. The skin should be brown and fuzzy.

Preparation: Always peel kiwis. Tropical fruits like kiwis are often imported from foreign countries where use of known carcinogenic sprays is still legal. Cut kiwis in half for juicing, in quarters for your blender. You can freeze kiwis; place kiwi chunks in a freezer bag and store in freezer until ready to use. They store well in the freezer for three to four weeks.

Nutritional content: Kiwis are rich in vitamin C and potassium. Vitamin C greatly increases the body's ability to use iron. It is recommended that you eat a vitamin C–rich food each time you eat an iron-rich food to gain maximum benefit.

LEMON The most common varieties of lemon are Eureka and Lisbon, followed by the Meyer and Villa Franca. The better-known Italian varieties are Little Monk and Turk's Head. California is the major producer of the world's lemons, with about 5 percent being grown in Italy.

Season: Lemons are available all year long, but peak months are April through August. Choose lemons that are deep yellow in color and firm but not hard. The skin should be slightly oily to the touch and thin for the most juice and flavor. Look for fruits that are heavy for their size. Avoid lemons that are shriveled, have hard skin, or are soft or spongy. Bypass lemons that are moldy, soft, or have discoloration at the stem.

Preparation: If a lemon is not organic, it should be peeled. The skin does have a very slight bitter taste, so I recommend that you peel all lemons to avoid any bitterness. Leave on as much of the white part just beneath the skin as possible, since that contains the most nutrients. A little freshly grated lemon zest can greatly enhance the flavor of your smoothies.

Nutritional content: Lemons are rich in vitamin C, potassium, and flavonoids, especially limonene.

Limonene has been shown to have anti-cancer effects and has been used to dissolve gallstones. The white part of the lemon is richest in vitamin C and flavonoids.

LIME The principal variety of lime grown in the United States is the Florida Persean. Florida is the top U.S. producer of limes, followed by California. Mexico grows limes as well.

Season: Limes can be found in the market year-round, but peak months are April through August. Choose limes that are bright green in color and firm but not hard. They should be heavy for their size and have a glossy, thin skin for the most juice and flavor.

Preparation: Peel limes that are not organically grown. I usually peel any lime, however, for the best-tasting juice and smoothies, since the skin can add a very slight bitter taste. However, a little freshly grated lime zest can greatly enhance the flavor of your smoothies.

Nutritional content: Limes are rich in vitamin C, flavonoids, and potassium. British sailors were known as "limeys" because they carried limes with them on long voyages to prevent scurvy. Though most of us don't worry about scurvy, vitamin C and flavonoids can strengthen gum tissue and prevent bleeding gums.

Mango The most popular variety of mango grown in the United States is the Hayden, which comes from Florida, the top producer of mangoes in the U.S. Other varieties sold here come from Haiti, the West Indies, and Mexico.

Season: Mangoes are available May through September, with a peak in June. Select mangoes that give a little when pressed slightly and are mottled with orange, gold, red, green, and black. Avoid solid green mangoes; they may never ripen. Bypass mangoes with extremely soft areas and black spots.

Preparation: Always peel a mango, since it may have come from a foreign country where the use of carcinogenic sprays is still legal. The best way is to make several top-to-bottom incisions all around the mango and peel the skin away as you would a banana. Slice the flesh away from the pit. Mangoes freeze well; place mango chunks in a freezer bag and store in the freezer until ready to use. You can keep the fruit in the freezer for three to four weeks.

Nutritional content: Mangoes are a good source of beta-carotene and potassium. The carotene content of human tissue is the most significant factor in determining maximal life span potential. To increase your intake of carotenes so you can live a long, healthy life, eat more orange, red, and dark green fruits and vegetables, which are rich in carotenes.

MELONS Popular melons include Persian, Casaba, Cranshaw, canary, honeydew, and cantaloupe. They belong to the gourd family and are related to watermelon and cucumbers. Melons are grown in the Southwest, particularly in California and Arizona.

Season: Cantaloupes are available May through September, with a peak in June and July. Honeydews are available year-round, with a peak from July through October. Choose melons that are firm, neither too soft nor too hard, and heavy for their size, which indicates juiciness. Cantaloupes should be cream colored and "netted." There should be a full scar at the stem end. Honeydew melons should be green, not white or greenish white, indicating immaturity.

Preparation: Peel the melon and discard the seeds, unless juicing it. The whole melon can be juiced, if it is organic. In this case, wash the skin well, and cut into pieces that will fit your juicer's feed tube. Melons can be frozen. Peel the melon and remove the seeds; cut it into one-inch chunks and place them in a freezer bag. Melon can be stored in the freezer three to four weeks.

Nutritional content: Cantaloupe, the most popular melon for smoothie recipes, is rich in beta-carotene, vitamin C, and potassium. Melons also contain adenosine, the same compound found in garlic and onions, which acts as an anticoagulant, helping thin the blood and lessening the risk of heart attack and stroke.

Orange There are over 200 varieties of oranges grown in the United States and three kinds: sweet, sour, and a group that includes tangerines, mandarins, and Satsumas. Sweet oranges are classified as normal, blood, or navel. Among the most popular sweet varieties are Washington Navel, Valencia, Hamlin, Indian River, and Jaffa. Florida and California are the top orange producers in the U.S.

Season: Oranges are available all year long, but their peak months are in the winter and spring. Select oranges that are firm and heavy for their size. The skin should be thin, smooth, and bright.

Preparation: Oranges should always be peeled because the skin contains a volatile oil that should not be consumed in large quantities. Leave as much of the white part on the orange as possible as it contains the most nutrients. A little freshly grated orange zest adds a lot of flavor to smoothies.

Nutritional content: Oranges are known for their vitamin C and flavonoids. Women who experience heavy bleeding during periods could benefit from these nutrients, since vitamin C and flavonoids work most effectively together to strengthen capillary walls and prevent heavy monthly bleeding. Oranges are also a good source of inositol and choline (B-complex vitamins), calcium, magnesium, potassium, manganese, and selenium.

PAPAYA Papaya is grown in California, Florida, and Texas, and in warm-climate areas of the world such as Mexico, West Indies, Asia, Africa, and Polynesia.

Season: Papayas are available year-round, but the peak months are May and June. Choose papayas that are golden orange or deep yellow; they should be somewhat soft but not mushy when ripe.

Preparation: Always peel a papaya, since this fruit, like all tropical fruits, often comes from countries that still use carcinogenic sprays. First, cut the papaya in half and scoop out the seeds. Then either remove the peel from the flesh or scoop the flesh from the peel. You can freeze papayas; simply cut the flesh into one-inch chunks and place them in a freezer bag. You can store them in the freezer for three to four weeks. To speed the ripening of a papaya, cut a thin portion from each end and make four full-length cuts from end to end, spacing them about one-quarter distance apart. Let the papaya sit at room temperature. In two or three days, the papaya should be ripe, unless it was picked too green.

Nutritional content: Papayas are a good source of beta-carotene and vitamin C and are best known for the protein-digesting enzyme papain, which has been used medicinally for such conditions as indigestion, inflammation, sports injuries, and allergies. Papain helps protect the stomach from ulcers caused by aspirin and steroids.

Parsley In the United States parsley comes in three varieties: common, with small leaves, Naples, with large leaves and thick stalks, and curly, with small leaves. Florida is the major U.S. producer, followed by California, Texas, and Arizona.

Season: Fresh parsley is available all year round, but peak season is October through December. Choose fresh, crisp, dark green parsley. Common and curly parsley should be springy. Avoid limp or yellowish parsley.

Preparation: Just wash parsley; immerse in cold water and shake the parsley to remove dirt and debris, then rinse and dry in a colander. If juicing, bunch it up and push through the juicer's feed tube. If placing it directly in a blender, chop it first. Parsley doesn't freeze well.

Nutritional content: Parsley is very rich in so many nutrients that it's almost a perfect food. Nutrients include beta-carotene, riboflavin (vitamin B2), vitamin C (very high), flavonoids, calcium, magnesium, phosphorus, potassium (very high), iron, zinc, and vanadium. It's also high in chlorophyll, a good blood purifier. It has been used medicinally and has been regarded as a nerve stimulant. No wonder juice enthusiasts label parsley-containing juices as "energy drinks."

Peach Peaches come in two types: clingstone, in which the flesh clings to the pit, and freestone, in which the pit is loose. The Alberta is the leading freestone variety; other popular varieties include Halehaven and Golden Jubilee. Clingstone peaches are grown mainly in California, while Georgia leads in production of the freestone, followed by Michigan and the Carolinas.

Season: Peaches are available May through October, but peak season is July and August. Buy fresh peaches only in season. Choose plump, slightly fuzzy peaches that are deep yellow or orange with a red blush. They should be firm but give slightly when pressed. Bypass overly green peaches; they may not ever be as sweet. Toward the end of the season in September and October, peaches can be quite mealy.

Preparation: Organic peaches need only be washed; peel nonorganic peaches. Cut them in half and remove the pit. Peaches can be frozen. Cut them in one-inch chunks and place them in a freezer bag. Frozen peaches can be stored three to four weeks.

Nutritional content: Peaches are a good source of the carotenoids—beta-carotene and zeaxanthin—flavonoids, and potassium. Zeaxanthin is especially protective of the macula of the retina, where it protects the photoreceptor cells from free-radical damage generated by light.

Pear Over 5,000 varieties of pears exist, but the Bartlett, Anjou, Bosc, and Seckel are the most popular varieties. They are grown primarily in California, Oregon, Washington, New York, and Michigan.

Season: Pears are available in most markets year-round, but varieties differ. Bartlett pears are a summer fruit, with peak season being July through November. In early autumn, the Seckel is available. The Anjou comes to market between October and May. Choose a pear that is deep-colored, plump, and firm but which yields when pressed. It should have a sweet fragrance when kept at room temperature. Avoid pears with extensive bruising; a little bruising is normal. Avoid mushy pears; they will have little juice.

Preparation: Organic pears need only be washed; nonorganic pears should be peeled. If juicing, cut them in pieces that will fit your juicer's feed tube. If adding them directly to your blender, remove the stem and seeds and cut the pear into chunks. Pears freeze well. Place pear chunks in a freezer bag; frozen pears can be stored three to four weeks.

Nutritional content: Pears are excellent sources of water-soluble fibers, especially pectins. One medium-size Bartlett pear contains nearly five grams of fiber. This type of fiber is especially good for regularity and colon health.

PINEAPPLE The most popular variety of pineapple is the Smooth Cayenne; other varieties include Red Spanish, Queen, and Pernambuco. The pineapple is still a symbol of hospitality and is grown all over the world, even in European hothouses, but it does best in tropical climates. Hawaii is the number one United States producer of pineapple.

Season: Pineapples are available year-round; peak season is March through July. Choose a pineapple that is large, plump, and firm with a fresh, clean appearance and a strong, sweet fragrance. Look for dark orange-yellow or golden color and fresh, deep green crown leaves. The eyes should be flat and hollow, with most of them at the base yellow. Bypass watery or dark eyes, brown leaves, and discolored or soft spots.

Preparation: Twist off the green-leaf top and peel the pineapple. Cut the pineapple into chunks for the blender or into spears for juicing. Pineapple freezes well. Cut it into chunks and place them in a freezer bag. Pineapple can be stored in the freezer for three to four weeks.

Nutritional content: Pineapple is a fairly good source of potassium, calcium, magnesium, iron, and iodine. Bromelain, the protein-digesting enzyme complex found in pineapple has been shown to be helpful for inflammatory conditions, indigestion, upper respiratory tract infections (especially sore throats), arthritis, and athletic injuries.

Plum and prune Plums can be found in all shades of blue, red, green, and yellow. The most popular varieties are the Damson Beauty, Italian Prune, Burbank, Sugar, and Stanley. California is the leading domestic producer of plums.

Season: Plums are available from June through September; peak time is July and August. Prunes are available year-round. Choose plums that yield to gentle pressure, have good color for the variety, and a slight glow to the skin. It is a bit of a challenge to find prunes that have not been treated with a sorbate preservative, since their sugars tend to rise to the surface, making them look moldy or frosted.

Preparation: Wash plums and cut them in half; remove the stones. Cut prunes into small pieces or make a prune puree by combining prunes in a blender with a little water on high speed.

Nutritional content: Plums contain some magnesium and are rich in flavonoids. Prunes are rich in beta-carotene, flavonoids, calcium, magnesium, phosphorus, and iron. Prunes are best known for their laxative effects.

Radish Radishes are loosely classified as either summer or winter variety: black, red, or white, and round or long-rooted. The most popular size is the cherry round red type. Domestically, most radishes are grown in California and Florida.

Season: Radishes are available year-round, but the peak months are April through June. Choose small, fresh radishes that are smooth and well formed. Look for smooth, tender, crisp radishes and avoid pithy or spongy ones. Bypass radishes with blemishes, sprouting, black spots, or cracks.

Preparation: Cut the greens off radishes and scrub.

Nutritional content: Radishes are rich in vitamin C, phosphorus, potassium, selenium, and vanadium. Most people don't take in enough selenium because of their diet or because of soil depletion. A deficiency of selenium is associated with heart disease and cancer.

Raspberry Raspberries are available in many varieties and colors. Yellow berries grow in Maryland, pink in Alabama and Oregon, lavender in North Carolina, and wild black raspberries with a deep wine color grow in the West. Purple berries are a hybrid of the black and red, and white berries grow wild.

Season: Raspberries are available from mid-April through mid-September, with July being the peak month. Choose berries that are bright, plump, and clean. Coloring should be full and solid, and the berries should be fresh and dry. Bypass berries that are dull, soft, or runny, and check the bottom of the container for moldy berries.

Preparation: Place the berries in a bowl of cold water and stir them gently with your hand or a wooden spoon. Drain the water and repeat; drain in a colander. Pick out any damaged berries. Raspberries can be frozen. Just let them dry in a colander and place them in a freezer bag. Berries can be stored in the freezer for several weeks.

Nutritional content: Raspberries are a good source of vitamin C, flavonoids, and potassium.

RHUBARB Rhubarb is grown throughout the United States and Europe. It is native to Tibet and North Asia.

Season: Rhubarb is available from January through June.

Preparation: Wash rhubarb under cold running water. Trim off the leaves, which are poisonous.

Nutritional content: Rhubarb is rich in calcium and potassium.

SPINACH There are several varieties of spinach, including flat and curly. Spinach is grown in the eastern and southern United States, especially Texas.

Season: Spinach is available all year long, but its peak months are April and May.

Preparation: Wash spinach well in cold water and then place it in a colander or salad spinner to drain. Chop it for the blender; simply bunch it up and push it through the feed tube for juicing.

Nutritional content: Spinach contains about twice as much iron as other greens and is also rich in beta-carotene, vitamin E, folic acid, vitamin B6, choline (one of the B-complex vitamins), vitamin C, calcium, magnesium, phosphorus, potassium, manganese, zinc, chromium, iodine, and nickel. It is also a good source of chlorophyll—a blood purifier. No wonder folklore imbues spinach with the remarkable ability to restore energy, increase vitality, and improve the quality of the blood.

STRAWBERRY Popular varieties of strawberries grown in the United States include Scarlet Virginia and Pocahontas. Other varieties include Blakemore, Klondike, Howard 17, and Marshall. Strawberries are grown in every state, including Alaska, but California, Oregon, and Washington are the top producers.

Season: Strawberries are available from January through September, with their peak from April through June. Look for firm, ripe dry berries that are fresh, clean, and shiny and a solid red color. Pick out any moldy berries. The best berries are locally grown, which are usually organic.

Preparation: Just rinse strawberries under cold running water and dry in a colander. Remove the caps if adding them to a blender; you can juice the caps. Strawberries can be frozen. Let them dry in a colander and place them in a freezer bag. They can be stored in the freezer for several weeks.

Nutritional content: Strawberries are a good source of inositol (one of the B-complex vitamins), vitamin C, flavonoids, potassium, and iron. Strawberries are also known for the cancer-fighting phytochemical ellagic acid.

TOMATO Numerous varieties of tomatoes are cultivated in the United States, including the cherry tomato, yellow pear, red Beefsteak, and Roma. Leading producers in the U.S. include California, Texas, Florida, Ohio, and Tennessee.

Season: Tomatoes are available year-round, but their peak season is May through September. Look for firm, plump, smooth tomatoes that are free of decay, cracks, or bruises. Avoid tomatoes with ridges at the stem end, since this is a sign of mealiness.

Preparation: Simply wash the tomatoes and cut them into chunks. Tomatoes freeze well. Place tomato chunks in a freezer bag; they can be stored in the freezer three to four weeks.

Nutritional content: Tomatoes supply fairly good amounts of vitamin C, carotenes, and potassium. Tomatoes are best known for lycopene, a carotene that has been extensively studied for its anti-cancer effects, especially in prostate cancer. Scientific studies showed men who ate the most servings of tomatoes (7 to 10 servings a week) had the least incidence of prostate cancer.

Binders and Other Special Ingredients

Almond milk Though not a true milk, almond milk tastes like milk and is sweet, with a slight almond flavor. Commercial brands typically have a thinner consistency much like that of skim milk. Almond milk has no cholesterol—the fat is monounsaturated, rich in oleic acid and vitamin E—and it also has a high calcium content, which makes it a good alternative to cow's milk, especially for people who are dairy sensitive. If you can't find almond milk at your supermarket or natural foods store, you can make it.

Almond Milk Recipe

2 cups blanched almonds
2 1/2 cups filtered water
1/4 cup brown rice syrup, pure maple syrup, or honey
2 teaspoons sea salt
1 teaspoon pure vanilla extract
1 teaspoon pure almond extract

Place almonds in a bowl and pour the water over them; soak overnight. Pour almonds and water in a blender or food processor and add the sweetener, salt, vanilla, and almond extract. Blend on high speed until completely smooth. Refrigerate until ready to use.

Makes about 5 cups

ALMONDS Almonds are a good source of protein. Throw a handful in your smoothie anytime you want to boost the protein content and thicken it a bit. They are a very rich source of vitamin E, calcium, magnesium, manganese, and potassium, and also offer substantial amounts of vitamins B1, B2, niacin, folic acid, biotin, phosphorus, iron, copper, zinc, and selenium.

BASIL Fresh sweet basil is especially good with tomato-based smoothies; the two are companion plants. It is also rich in essential oils. Sweet basil can be found in the herb section of most supermarkets year-round.

BRAN Bran is the outer layer of wheat, rye, or oats, for example, removed by the milling process. It is a good source of fiber and a worthy supplement in one's diet, especially when the intake of whole grains is insufficient. Bran helps to regulate the gastrointestinal tract, and it is a good source of vitamins E, B1, and B2, niacin, folic acid, biotin, choline, calcium, magnesium, phosphorus, iron, and selenium. You can add a tablespoon of bran to most of the fruit smoothies in this book, and its sweet, nutty flavor will blend well with the other ingredients.

CAROB With a color and consistency similar to that of cocoa, carob is a tasty alternative to chocolate. Though this powder ground from pods of the Mediterranean evergreen tree does not taste like chocolate, it has a pleasant, sweet taste that many people find enjoyable. Being naturally sweet, it does not need additional sugar. Unlike chocolate, it contains no caffeine and very little fat. (Chocolate also contains compounds that can contribute to migraines, acne, heartburn, and fibrocystic breast disease.) Carob is one of the richest sources of calcium nature offers. Carob and banana mix well together for a smoothie that looks and tastes a bit like a cocoa milk shake.

CASHEWS When you want to add a binding, thickening agent without using dairy or bananas, raw cashews are an excellent choice. A handful of these nuts will make any smoothie creamier, while at the same time adding protein. Nearly all cashew processing takes place in India, and each kernel is removed by hand, therefore, cashews may experience less of the negative effects of machine processing than most other nuts. Cashews are a good source of vitamins B1 and B2, pantothenic acid, calcium, magnesium, phosphorus, and iron.

FLAXSEED AND FLAXSEED OIL Flaxseed and flaxseed oil taste good, rather nutty when fresh, and both combine well in most smoothie recipes. The seeds are useless to the body when eaten whole, because their hard coating causes them to pass right through intact, with no nutritional benefits realized. And the nutritional benefits of the seeds (and oil) are numerous. Therefore, whenever possible, add some flaxseed to your smoothie and the blender will grind it up, or pour in a tablespoon of the oil. Flax is one of the richest sources of unsaturated alpha-linolenic fatty acids available. A unique feature of flaxseed is that it contains a substance resembling prostaglandins that regulates blood pressure, platelet, kidney, immune, and arterial function, and inflammatory response, and play important roles in calcium and energy metabolism. Flax oil contains lecithin, which helps emulsify fats and oils for easier digestion. It also contains carotenes, vitamin E, protein, some B vitamins, and trace amounts of manganese, silicon, copper, fluorine, nickel, cobalt, iodine, molybdenum, and chromium. In addition, it is one of nature's best sources of lignans—molecules with antifungal, antiviral, antibacterial, and anti-cancer functions. Buy only refrigerated, cold-pressed flaxseed oil, available in many supermarkets and most natural food stores. The oil should always be refrigerated and lasts two to four weeks. It can also be frozen.

Herbal tea Herbal teas can be frozen in ice cube trays and added to your favorite smoothie combinations. I've added a number of different herbal teas, such as peppermint, chai, peach, chamomile, and Red Zinger to recipes, changing and adding rich flavor. The nutritional benefits of various herbal teas are as varied as the flavors. From the benefits of better digestion from peppermint to the relaxing, calming effects of chamomile, you'll enjoy healthful as well as flavorful bonuses from herbal tea smoothies.

Honey Many of the recipes in this book call for honey, especially the desserts. The most common types of honey are clover and alfalfa, which are mild in flavor and light-colored; buckwheat is dark and robust; wildflower is somewhere in between. Other varieties include orange blossom, tupelo, safflower, sage, heather, and thyme. Avoid brands whose commercially raised bees are fed sugar water or corn syrup. Look for unheated, unfiltered, unprocessed honey. Honey is a concentrated source of sugars, but unlike the empty calories of refined sugar, it contains amino acids, B-complex vitamins, vitamins C, D, and E, and some minerals. Diabetics and hypoglycemics should use very little honey, since blood sugar reacts to it as it would to refined sugar. Children under two years of age should *not ever* be fed honey, even pasteurized brands, since it can transmit heat-resistant botulism spores that can be life-threatening; substitute pure maple syrup. These do not affect older children or adults.

MAPLE SYRUP Less sweet than honey, pure maple syrup is a good alternative to honey for those who are sensitive to sugars. It adds a delicious flavor to smoothies—one I prefer. Maple syrup comes in different grades, which are mostly related to temperature and time of process. Grade A maple syrups are generally lighter in color and flavor, while Grade B is darker in color and stronger in flavor. Pure maple syrup imported from Canada may be more "pure" than U.S. brands because some producers here use formaldehyde pellets to keep tapholes open but are not required to list this on the label. Look for labels that indicate that the syrup has no added salt, chemical preservatives, or defoamers. Completely avoid pancake syrup, which is a blend of corn syrup and artificial flavors.

Milk Milk is made up of protein in the form of casein and whey, water, lactose, fat, vitamins, and minerals—vitamin D, riboflavin, calcium, magnesium, and potassium. Though it is a nutritious food, many people are sensitive to dairy products and suffer ear infections, sinus infections, reduced immunity, and other adverse reactions because of its consumption. One of the reasons may be that human beings are the only animals that continue to drink milk way beyond infancy, even though the lactose enzyme wanes as we grow older. Also, the high fat content is not something that is good for anybody. If you do choose cow's milk for your smoothies, choose nonfat milk or acidophilus milk. For those sensitive to the protein components of cow's milk, goat's milk may be a viable alternative, since incidence of intolerance is low compared with that of cow's milk. My recommendation for the least incidence of intolerance is soy milk, almond milk, or rice milk.

Mint Fresh mint adds a refreshing touch to fruit-based smoothies and frozen desserts. It is also quite helpful for indigestion and colds. It's effective for colic and flatulence. Its flavonoids stimulate the gallbladder and liver, increasing the flow of bile, and it is known to aid digestion and soothe a tummy ache. Fresh mint is available year-round in the herb section of most supermarkets.

PEANUT BUTTER Not actually nuts, but legumes, peanuts are a source of protein, vitamin E, vitamin B1, niacin, pantothenic acid, folic acid, biotin, inositol, choline, calcium, magnesium, phosphorus, iron, copper, manganese, zinc, and iodine. Choose peanut butter that has no added oil, sugar, salt, or additives. To keep the nut butter from separating, stabilizers such as hydrogenated oil or mono- and diglycerides are often added to save you the trouble of mixing the oil at the top with the rest of the peanut butter. Avoid these brands—none of these additives is good for you; choose only "all-natural" or "old-fashioned" nut butters, as they are often referred to, which contain only ground peanuts. You can add a scoop of peanut butter to most smoothies and it will taste good; it goes especially well with banana.

SESAME SEEDS AND TAHINI (SESAME BUTTER) Sesame seeds are an excellent source of calcium and also offer vitamin E, niacin, phosphorus, iron, and trace amounts of vitamins B1 and B2. In addition, they contain some lignans and other cancer-fighting phytochemicals. Tahini is a spread made from ground sesame seeds and is also known as sesame butter. This seed puree is a common ingredient in Middle Eastern cuisine. Most brands are free of additives; organically grown sesame seeds and tahini are also available.

SOFT SILKEN TOFU Tofu is a soybean curd made by separating out the protein in soy milk, using a mineral coagulant. Soft silken tofu is sweeter, with a higher water content and a custard-like texture. It is best for smoothies and desserts, and can usually be found in the refrigerator section of your supermarket. It is a rich source of protein, with no saturated fat or cholesterol. It contains lecithin, which can help to lower dangerously high blood pressure. Lecithin is also indicated as a lipotropic agent, meaning it promotes the utilization of fat. Thus soy is often incorporated in weight-loss products. Additionally, soybeans contain stigmasterol, an anti-stiffness factor. Sitosterol, a by-product of soy, has been used to replace some components of antihypertensive drugs. The most intriguing and promising components of soy are the isoflavones—genistein, daidzein, and glycitein—which function similarly to human estrogen. Estrogen is key to healthy functioning of the female endocrine and reproductive systems. Isoflavones exert a balancing effect on hormonal levels, balancing excesses and deficiencies. They have also demonstrated anti-carcinogenic and anti-angiogenic characteristics. They have compounds similar to human steroids and have been proved to boost the immune system and benefit the heart. New research also indicates that the isoflavone daidzein may help to stop calcium loss from human bones and thereby prevent osteoporosis.

SOY MILK Soy milk is a nondairy alternative made by grinding soybeans to a flour-like consistency, cooking the "flour" in water, and pressing out the liquid. Soy milks are commercially distributed in flexible foil-like aseptic cartons that can be kept at room temperature until ready to use. Once opened, the carton must be refrigerated. Soy milk is available in plain, vanilla, chocolate, and carob. Some companies add oil to give it more body; avoid these. Some brands are sweetened with honey, brown rice syrup, barley malt, or maple syrup. The label may also indicate the addition of kombu (a seaweed) that is harmless and is used to enhance flavor and consistency, as well as carrageenan and vegetable gums. You can make your own soy milk. Salton, Inc. has an inexpensive soy milk maker that will allow you to make your own fresh, additive-free soy milk any time you wish. The benefits are similar to that of tofu, noted above.

Stevia A natural plant extract that contains no calories, stevia is an ideal sweetener for anyone who wants to reduce calories and especially for sugar-sensitive individuals such as hypoglycemics, diabetics, and people with yeast problems. It is one of the few sweeteners available that does not raise blood sugar levels; therefore, it is good for sustained energy levels. Stevia is very sweet and you will need only about 1/8 teaspoon for a smoothie recipe. It is available in powdered and liquid forms at most natural food stores.

Sunflower seeds Sunflower seeds and sunflower seed butter add a fresh, nutty flavor to smoothies. They also add an abundance of protein, and sunflower seeds top the charts on most nutrients, including vitamin E, vitamins B1, B2, and B6, niacin, pantothenic acid, calcium, magnesium, phosphorus, potassium, iron, and vanadium. Choose clean, plump sunflower seeds of fairly uniform shape and color. Sometimes color can be misleading because of a chemical "whitewashing." Avoid seeds with a blackening surface, a sign of decay. If possible to sample, choose seeds that are crunchy and fresh; avoid seeds that are limp or rubbery—they're on the decline. If they burn your tongue or throat, they are rancid.

Yogurt Yogurt adds a nice tart taste to smoothies and is an excellent thickener. You can use dairy yogurt or soy yogurt, although I have found that soy yogurt has quite an overpowering taste in most of the smoothie recipes. Many people who are lactose intolerant and unable to use milk can tolerate dairy yogurt. Plain, unflavored dairy yogurt will be the most versatile for your recipes, as it will blend best with the delicious taste of fruit and other flavorings. If you choose a truly natural yogurt that has live cultures of healthful bacteria such as *Lactobacillus bulgaricus* or *Lactobacillus acidophilus,* the bacteria will promote the growth of healthy microflora in the intestinal tract. It is especially important to eat yogurt after taking antibiotics or experiencing diarrhea to replenish the good bacteria in the gut, and a smoothie is an excellent way to consume this beneficial food. Additionally, yogurt offers protein, some B vitamins, and calcium. Look for yogurt that contains only live cultures; avoid products with modified food starch, guar gum, locust bean gum, carob bean gum, carrageenan, and refined thickeners.

Flavor Extracts

Flavor extracts are a great addition to smoothies, enhancing flavor without calories. They are usually sold in two forms—pure extracts and imitation flavors. Pure extracts offer real flavor essences from the vanilla bean, almond, or raspberry, for example, diluted with ingredients such as glycerin, ethyl alcohol, or vegetable oil. Imitation flavors are chemical compounds that simulate the taste of the real flavor. They may also contain dyes to make them resemble the real product. I don't recommend imitation flavors because they are chemical based; chemicals are not health promoting. Pure vanilla, lemon, orange, and almond extracts can be found at most supermarkets. Look for other pure extracts, such as anise, coconut, and raspberry, at your natural food store. The brand of pure extracts I use is Frontier.

Nutritional Supplements

Any of the supplements in this section can be added to your smoothies—from a teaspoon to a tablespoon—without changing the flavor in most instances, but enhancing the nutritional value.

Acidophilus Acidophilus is the good bacteria known as *Lactobacillus acidophilus, Lactobacillus bulgaricus* and *Bifidobacterium bifidum* that populate the intestinal tract. They digest proteins, a process that produces lactic acid, enzymes, antibiotic substances, and B vitamins. A healthy colon should have mostly *lactobacillus,* with only a small percentage of *coliform* bacteria; however, the typical colon colony is the reverse. This results in excess gas, bloating, intestinal discomfort, toxicity, constipation, and malabsorption of nutrients, which leads to an overgrowth of yeast known as *Candida* and parasites. Acidophilus can help to detoxify the colon because the good bacteria bind with some of the unfriendly substances, causing them to be excreted. Acidophilus should always be taken following antibiotics, diarrhea, or if you have candidiasis or parasites. Acidophilus comes in both liquid and powdered forms and can be found at most natural food stores. Keep it in the refrigerator at all times, since the friendly bacteria can die at warmer temperatures. Do not freeze. It works best taken on an empty stomach, but if you have trouble getting yourself or someone else to take it, then add it to a smoothie.

Ascorbic acid (vitamin C powder) Vitamin C powder can be added to any smoothie without changing the flavor. It is an antioxidant that scavenges free radicals and is needed for tissue growth and repair as well as for proper adrenal gland function and healthy gums. It protects the body against infections, bolsters the immune system, and helps prevent cancer. Essential in the formation of collagen, it is an anti-aging nutrient. It prevents easy bruising and excess bleeding, and is especially helpful for women with heavy menses, strengthening capillary walls to prevent easy bleeding.

Vitamin C promotes wound healing and the synthesis of antistress hormones. The body cannot manufacture vitamin C; it must be obtained through the diet. Most people don't eat enough vitamin C–rich vegetables and fruits; therefore, vitamin C supplementation is highly advisable. You can get your daily dose of vitamin C by adding the appropriate measurement of ascorbic acid to your favorite smoothie. My favorite brand of ascorbic acid powder is manufactured by Pure Encapsulations.

Bee pollen A fine, powdery material produced by flowering plants, pollen is gathered by bees. Added to smoothies, it doesn't change the taste at all, just the nutritional content. It is highly nutritious, containing B-complex vitamins, vitamin C, amino acids, polyunsaturated fatty acids, enzymes, carotenes, calcium, copper, iron, magnesium, potassium, manganese, sodium, and protein. If you can find local bee pollen, it is said to help seasonal allergies. Look for it in the refrigerator section of natural food stores.

Echinacea A bitter herb that is used for colds, flu, infections, and colic, it has antiviral, antibiotic, and anti-inflammatory properties. It is good for the immune, glandular, and lymphatic systems. Echinacea contains enzymes, fatty acids, iron, protein, sulfur, vitamins C and E, and a host of phytochemicals. The best forms to add to a smoothie are dried or liquid.

GINSENG Categorized as an herb, ginseng comes in three varieties: Siberian, American, and Panax. It is suggested for colds, chest pains, impotence (stimulates male sex glands), stress (strengthens the adrenal glands), energy, diabetes, radiation protection, and lung protection. It enhances immune functions and helps normalize blood pressure. The best form for adding to smoothies is the liquid extract that can be found at most natural food stores.

GOLDENSEAL A bitter herb, goldenseal is popularly used to strengthen the immune system. It is good for colds, flu, inflammation, and infections. It has antibacterial and anti-inflammatory properties and acts as an antibiotic. The best form of goldenseal for smoothies is the liquid, or tincture form. It has a rather strong taste, but typically you would add only a few drops, which wouldn't noticeably affect the flavor.

LECITHIN Supplemental lecithin is derived from soybeans or egg yolks. It protects cells from oxidation and feeds the protective sheaths surrounding the brain, which are composed of lecithin. The muscle and nerve cells also contain this essential fatty acid. Lecithin is made up primarily of the B vitamin choline and also contains inositol and linoleic acid. Lecithin acts as a fat emulsifier, thereby helping to prevent cardiovascular disease. It helps increase brain functions and promotes energy. It comes in two forms appropriate for smoothies, liquid and granules, and won't change the smoothie flavor in the slightest. I recommend soy lecithin. It will spoil easily, so it must be refrigerated at all times. Do not freeze.

Milk thistle Also known as silymarin, milk thistle is a potent liver cleanser and restorer. It contains some of the most potent liver-protecting substances known. It is helpful for all liver disorders, such as jaundice and hepatitis, and it stimulates the production of new liver cells. Additionally, it protects the kidneys. This herb would be especially helpful to add to the Hangover Helper smoothie (page 143), and excellent for anyone to use to promote healthy liver function. The powdered variety is preferred over the alcohol-based extracts.

Minerals The combined factors of nutrient-depleted agricultural soils from centuries of overuse and synthetic fertilizers that force crops to grow rapidly with less nutrient absorption result in less and less mineral content in our food. Our bodies are made up of minerals, and we cannot manufacture them; we must ingest them. Minerals are required for appropriate biological functions and electrical conductivity. When imbalances and deficiencies of minerals occur, we experience illness, disease, and disorder. It is easy to add a tablespoon or two of liquid minerals to your smoothie; and especially if you have a brand that does not have an unpleasant taste, you'll never know they are present, but your body will reap the health benefits. I recommend a brand by Eniva that does not have an overpowering taste. You can order by calling 1-800-253-7474.

PROTEIN POWDER Adding protein powder to your smoothie makes it a complete meal, with the benefits of stabilizing blood sugar and counteracting what might otherwise be too much insulin release because of the fruit sugars, but without the fat and cholesterol contained in animal protein. Protein powder is typically made from cow's milk, goat's milk, eggs, or soybeans, with added vitamins, minerals, enzymes, phytonutrients, and fiber. I recommend soy-based protein powders because of soy's remarkable health benefits. (See Soft Silken Tofu, page 54). I have my own protein powder, the Juice Lady's Energy Formula, which is soy based; it is sweetened with fructooligosaccharides (good for colon health) and contains grain and sprout fiber, an abundance of phytonutrients, vitamins, minerals, and friendly bacteria for the colon. It's the formula I had always wanted and couldn't find, so I designed it myself. It's not available at this time in most stores, but you can order it by calling Salton at 1-888-889-0899 or visit www.salton.maxim.com. You may also order the Juice Lady juicer, Juice Lady blender, and other Juice Lady products made by Salton through this number.

Spirulena The most popular of the microalgae, spirulena is an excellent food source. It contains a high amount of protein, gamma-linolenic acid, high amounts of vitamin B12 (excellent for vegetarians), high iron content, amino acids, chlorophyll, and phycocyanin, a pigment that has anti-cancer properties. It protects the immune system, reduces cholesterol, and aids in mineral absorption. It also helps to curb appetite and stabilize blood sugar, making it an excellent addition for weight-loss programs.

UDO's Choice Beyond Greens is made from whole foods, food concentrates, and herbal extracts. It contains seeds rich in omega-3 and omega-6 fatty acids, green foods rich in chlorophyll, fiber, enzymes, and vegetable and herbal extracts. It can be found at many health food stores.

Recipes

When I thought about who could help me create some of the most delicious smoothie recipes on earth, I knew it had to be friend and co-author of my book *Cooking for Life* Vicki Chelf. Vicki came to our home in the mountains of Colorado and together we concocted smoothies that made us both say yum, wow, fabulous! My husband—our faithful taste tester—responded similarly. I think you'll agree, too—they're some of the best.

We had a number of five-star favorites, such as Chai Smoothie (page 101), Curb Your Cravings (page 119), Tummy Soother (page 125), and Anise Ice (page 311). Try them and see what you think.

I developed theme sections so you could easily find a smoothie recipe for your individual needs. Meals-in-a-Glass (page 72) has a number of breakfast smoothies that make complete meals, just as the title suggests, such as The Health Nut (page 77). Coffee-Break Shakes and Smoothies (page 88) offers delicious alternatives to coffee and sugary snacks; try Peachy Morning (page 103). Terrific Health-and-Healing Smoothies suggests healthful ingredients for a variety of conditions such as bone-strengthening (page 123), digestion-healing (page 131), and immune-boosting shakes (page 133). Workout and Bodybuilding Smoothies (page 158) blends nutrients to power muscles with Muscle Power Plus (page 163) or energize with High-Power Workout (page 167). Replace electrolytes with Competition Gator Shake (page 169). There are No-Fat Weight-Loss Helpers (page 182), Healthful Smoothies, Shakes, and Popsicles Kids Love (page 202), Healthy-Pregnancy Smoothies and New-Parent Pick-Me-Uppers (page 232), and so much more to keep you eating healthfully, even when you're on the run.

NOTE: Nutritional analyses are per serving, **NOT** per recipe.

Nutrisips

To make the nutrition information that accompanies my recipes as fun and accessible as possible, I've included "Nutrisips," tips on the nutritional benefits of one or more of the ingredients in a recipe. That way you can enjoy the smoothie or dessert twice as much, knowing what you are contributing to your own or someone else's well-being.

Storage Tips for Smoothies

- Drink smoothies made with ice right away. Other smoothies can be stored in the refrigerator or taken with you in a thermos, and should keep up to 24 hours.
- Want to perk up a stored smoothie? Pour the mixture into a blender, add a few ice cubes, and blend.
- You can freeze smoothies into yummy sorbets, sherbets, and ices. For most smoothie recipes, add one to three tablespoons of honey or pure maple syrup, or sweeten as desired, and blend the frozen mixture in a food processor before serving. Frozen smoothie desserts can be stored in the freezer several weeks. (See Just Desserts for complete recipes, page 304. Many of the smoothies make great popsicles as well. See Healthful Smoothies, Shakes, and Popsicles Kids Love, page 202.)

Meals-in-a-Glass and Toppings for Your Health

Eating breakfast is important for the health of children in particular but for adults, too. Survey data from the National Health and Nutrition Examination Survey II showed that cholesterol levels are lowest among people who eat cereal for breakfast. People who consumed other breakfast foods had higher cholesterol levels, but surprisingly, levels were the highest among those who totally skipped breakfast.

Whole-grain cereals are among the healthiest choices you can make for breakfast. Whole grains offer an abundance of vitamin E, many of the B vitamins, and a host of minerals. They are low in fat, contain no saturated fat or cholesterol, and are high in fiber. Grains such as oats can go right into your breakfast smoothie, making it a healthy start for your day.

In our hurry to embrace low-carbohydrate, high-protein diets, wisdom would tell us to remember our arteries and that most animal proteins contain saturated fat. We might be shedding a few pounds but clogging up our blood vessels. Scientific studies still stand true—oat bran and flaxseed work to lower cholesterol and triglycerides. They're also good for the colon, and they aren't fattening. I eat whole grains with ground flaxseed most mornings; they're part of the routine that helps me stay slim and trim.

Making a hot breakfast in the morning may seem difficult to squeeze into your morning routine. That's why breakfast smoothies make such good sense. You can partially prepare ingredients the night before by soaking the seeds, nuts, and grains with fruit juice or soy milk, for example. In the morning, you need only pour the mixture into your blender and add the remaining items. In just a few minutes you'll have a delicious, healthy breakfast meal-in-a-glass that you can sip as you prepare for your day or ride to work.

On days when you do have the time to prepare a hot cereal, the toppings in this section will add delicious flavor and additional nutrients. Double the recipe and you'll have enough for the next morning as well. Also, the Umebushi Plum Tofu Topping (page 87) is really great on soups, stir-fry, even corn bread. We've topped borscht with it instead of sour cream in our home and thought it tasted better than the high-fat dairy we'd been used to eating. We spread it on fresh-baked corn bread instead of butter and love the flavor.

Rhubarb Raisin Morning

Total Weight:	17.8 oz.	Serving Size:	8.9 oz.

Serves 2

BASIC COMPONENTS			
Calories	234.6	Vitamin E	1.5 IU
Calories from fat	119.3	Folate	35.6 mcg
Protein	7.2 g	MINERALS	
Carbohydrates	26.6 g	Calcium	76.0 mg
Dietary fiber	6.0 g	Iron	2.1 mg
Sugar—total	12.9 g	Magnesium	82.3 mg
Fat—total	13.3 g	Potassium	371.0 mg
Saturated fat	1.8 g	Selenium	5.9 mcg
Monounsaturated fat	2.0 g	Sodium	23.7 mg
Polyunsaturated fat	6.6 g	Zinc	1.5 mg
VITAMINS		OTHER FATS	
A—beta-carotene	15.7 mcg	Omega-3 fatty acids	2.3 g
Vitamin B6	0.2 mg	Omega-6 fatty acids	4.3 g
Vitamin C	4.1 mg		

Stewed Rhubarb and Raisins

This fruit sauce tastes great over cooked cereal as well as in the Rhubarb Raisin Morning smoothie (page 75).

3 cups tender rhubarb, diced (1/2-inch dice; discard all leaves, as they are toxic)
1 cup raisins
1/2 cup orange juice
2 tablespoons honey or pure maple syrup
1 teaspoon grated orange peel, preferably organic

Combine all the ingredients in a saucepan and heat slowly over medium heat, occasionally stirring gently with a rubber spatula, until it begins to boil. Lower the heat and simmer the mixture, stirring it gently until the fruit is tender, about 30 minutes. Add more sweetener to taste.

Rhubarb Raisin Morning

Rhubarb is rarely eaten raw, and with cooking, sweetener needs to be added; then it's delicious. It adds a nice flavor and consistency to this smoothie.

Nutrisip: Rhubarb and raisins are a good source of calcium, and raisins are also high in magnesium, manganese, phosphorus, potassium, and iron. When you combine raisins with orange juice, which is rich in vitamin C, as in the Stewed Rhubarb and Raisins, you will absorb much more iron. Vitamin C facilitates a much higher iron absorption.

1/2 cup Stewed Rhubarb and Raisins (see box on opposite page for stewing instructions)
1/4 cup rolled oats
2 tablespoons flaxseed
1 cup plain soy milk or milk of choice
1 tablespoon soy lecithin granules
1/2 teaspoon ground cloves
1/8 teaspoon stevia or 1 tablespoon pure maple syrup
6 ice cubes

Place the rhubarb and raisin mixture in a bowl with the oats and flaxseed and cover with the soy milk. Cover the bowl and place in the refrigerator overnight. Pour the mixture into a blender and add the lecithin, cloves, sweetener, and ice cubes. Blend on high speed for about one minute or until completely blended. Pour into bowls and serve immediately.

The Health Nut

Total Weight:	22.2 oz.	Serving Size:	11.1 oz.

Serves 2

Basic Components

Calories	297.0
Calories from fat	135.2
Protein	10.6 g
Carbohydrates	24.5 g
Dietary fiber	3.8 g
Sugar—total	13.2 g
Fat—total	15.0 g
Saturated fat	1.3 g
Monounsaturated fat	6.6 g
Polyunsaturated fat	4.8 g

Vitamins

A—beta-carotene	982.5 mcg
Vitamin B6	0.2 mg
Vitamin C	70.0 mg
Vitamin E	10.0 IU
Folate	85.1 mcg

Minerals

Calcium	117.7 mg
Iron	11.8 mg
Magnesium	98.3 mg
Potassium	611.2 mg
Selenium	4.3 mcg
Sodium	63.3 mg
Zinc	1.6 mg

Other Fats

Omega-3 fatty acids	0.9 g
Omega-6 fatty acids	3.7 g

The Health Nut

This particular smoothie has been one of my favorite morning drinks for several years. I love the taste of the parsley and pineapple juice blended with the nuts.

Nutrisip: Parsley is rich in vitamin C, bioflavonoids, beta-carotene, iron, calcium, magnesium, potassium, zinc, and vanadium. Couple that with bromelain from the pineapple juice and protein and essential fatty acids from the nuts, and you have a complete meal-in-a-glass. Talk about a morning energizer! This smoothie will give you the energy you need for a physical workout or challenging mental work.

1 cup pineapple juice (juice half a pineapple, if making fresh)
10 almonds, whole or blanched
1 tablespoon sunflower seeds
1 tablespoon sesame seeds
1 tablespoon flaxseed
1 cup chopped parsley
1/2 cup plain soy milk or milk of choice
1/2 teaspoon pure vanilla extract
1 tablespoon protein powder
6 ice cubes

Place the nuts, seeds, and pineapple juice in a bowl, cover, and soak overnight. Place this nut and seed mixture with the juice in the blender and add the parsley, soy milk, vanilla, protein powder, and ice cubes. Blend on high speed until smooth. This drink will be a bit chewy because of the nuts and seeds.

To kill molds, soak nuts and dried fruit for one hour to overnight in water and 1/2 teaspoon ascorbic acid.

Muesli-in-a-Glass

Total Weight:	18.8 oz.	Serving Size:	9.4 oz.

Serves 2

Basic Components			
Calories	334.3	Folate	51.8 mcg
Calories from fat	90.0	**Minerals**	
Protein	11.5 g	Calcium	71.9 mg
Carbohydrates	55.3 g	Iron	3.6 mg
Dietary fiber	9.0 g	Magnesium	94.1 mg
Sugar—total	30.1 g	Potassium	608.0 mg
Fat—total	10.0 g	Selenium	11.6 mcg
Saturated fat	1.5 g	Sodium	19.6 mg
Monounsaturated fat	1.9 g	Zinc	2.2 mg
Polyunsaturated fat	5.7 g	**Other Fats**	
Vitamins		Omega-3 fatty acids	1.8 g
A—beta-carotene	10.5 mcg	Omega-6 fatty acids	3.8 g
Vitamin B6	0.4 mg		
Vitamin C	509.4 mg		
Vitamin E	8.9 IU		

Muesli-in-a-Glass

I often eat muesli when I travel in Europe, and this smoothie reminds me of my bowls of yogurt, oats, nuts, and dried fruit I so enjoy when I'm there. The good part about this muesli is that you can take it with you as you leave home and sip it on your ride to work.

Nutrisip: Oats are a good source of many of the B vitamins and vitamin E as well as the trace minerals manganese, zinc, selenium, nickel, molybdenum, and vanadium. Oats contain gluten (omit if gluten sensitive) and phytates, a binding agent that can cause some mineral losses if consumed frequently. That is why soaking grains overnight, as recommended here, is such a wise idea. It breaks down some of the phytic acid in the bran.

1/2 cup raisins
1/4 cup rolled oats
2 tablespoons sunflower seeds
2 tablespoons flaxseed
2 tablespoons bee pollen
1/2 teaspoon ascorbic acid (vitamin C powder)
1/2 cup plain or vanilla soy milk
1/2 cup unsweetened applesauce
1/2 teaspoon cinnamon extract or ground cinnamon
6 ice cubes

Place raisins, oats, sunflower seeds, flaxseed, bee pollen, and ascorbic acid in a bowl and cover with soy milk. Cover the bowl and let soak overnight in the refrigerator. Pour the applesauce into a blender and add the raisin-oat mixture, cinnamon, and ice cubes. Blend on high speed for about one minute or until completely blended. Pour into a glass and eat with a straw.

Babylonian Breakfast

Total Weight:	16.7 oz.	Serving Size:	8.3 oz.

Serves 2

Basic Components

Calories	275.8
Calories from fat	90.9
Protein	13.4 g
Carbohydrates	36.0 g
Dietary fiber	6.5 g
Sugar—total	22.3 g
Fat—total	10.1 g
Saturated fat	2.1 g
Monounsaturated fat	3.5 g
Polyunsaturated fat	3.7 g

Vitamins

A—beta-carotene	1.2 mcg
Vitamin B6	0.2 mg
Vitamin C	6.9 mg
Vitamin E	2.9 IU
Folate	49.0 mcg

Minerals

Calcium	273.6 mg
Iron	2.0 mg
Magnesium	106.8 mg
Potassium	670.8 mg
Selenium	8.9 mcg
Sodium	102.3 mg
Zinc	2.2 mg

Other Fats

Omega-3 fatty acids	1.9 g
Omega-6 fatty acids	1.8 g

Babylonian Breakfast

"Drinkable breads" have been part of nearly all civilizations. Return to your ancient roots by drinking your morning grains in a very traditional mixture of grains, seeds, nuts, and yogurt like a true Babylonian.

Nutrisip: Flaxseed is rich in omega-3 fatty acids and is one of the richest sources of lignans. To release these heart-healthy nutrients from the hard coating of the flaxseed, it must be ground in a blender or nut grinder. Otherwise, the flaxseed will pass right through your body without any benefit to you at all.

1/4 cup rolled oats
1/4 cup raisins
2 tablespoons almonds
2 tablespoons flaxseed
1/2 cup plain soy milk or milk of choice
1 cup plain low-fat yogurt
1 tablespoon fresh lemon juice
1 teaspoon freshly grated lemon peel, preferably organic

Place the oats, raisins, almonds, and flaxseed in a bowl and pour the soy milk over them. Cover the bowl and refrigerate overnight. Pour the oat mixture into a blender and add the yogurt, lemon juice, and lemon peel. Blend on high speed until smooth. Serve immediately.

Lemon Prune Whipped Cereal Topping

Total Weight:	11.2 oz.	Serving Size:	2.8 oz.

Serves 4

Basic Components

Calories	72.4
Calories from fat	9.2
Protein	3.6 g
Carbohydrates	12.7 g
Dietary fiber	1.0 g
Sugar—total	9.9 g
Fat—total	1.0 g
Saturated fat	0.6 g
Monounsaturated fat	0.3 g
Polyunsaturated fat	0.0 g

Vitamins

A—beta-carotene	136.1 mcg
Vitamin B6	0.1 mg
Vitamin C	3.3 mg
Vitamin E	0.3 IU
Folate	7.9 mcg

Minerals

Calcium	119.2 mg
Iron	0.4 mg
Magnesium	16.7 mg
Potassium	242.6 mg
Selenium	2.3 mcg
Sodium	43.6 mg
Zinc	0.6 mg

Other Fats

Omega-3 fatty acids	0.0 g
Omega-6 fatty acids	0.0 g

poog

Lemon Prune Whipped Cereal Topping

Instead of milk, enjoy the great flavor of a lemon-flavored fruit topping on your morning cereal. It is simply delicious over any cooked cereal, such as oatmeal, millet, or cream of rice.

Nutrisip: Prunes are a good source of vitamin B6, beta-carotene, bioflavonoids, calcium, magnesium, and phosphorus.

1 cup plain low-fat yogurt
6 prunes, soft or stewed
1 tablespoon fresh lemon juice
1 teaspoon freshly grated lemon peel, preferably organic
1 teaspoon pure vanilla extract

Combine the yogurt in a blender with the prunes, lemon juice, lemon peel, and vanilla. Blend on high speed until smooth. Use immediately or refrigerate until ready to use. Spoon the mixture over your cereal and enjoy a flavorful treat.

Apricot Creme Topping

Total Weight: 24.1 oz. Serving Size: 12.0 oz.

Serves 2

Basic Components		Vitamin E	2.7 IU
Calories	223.2	Folate	15.9 mcg
Calories from fat	39.0	**Minerals**	
Protein	8.8 g	Calcium	62.2 mg
Carbohydrates	40.8 g	Iron	2.1 mg
Dietary fiber	4.8 g	Magnesium	53.1 mg
Sugar—total	33.4 g	Potassium	776.3 mg
Fat—total	4.3 g	Selenium	1.3 mcg
Saturated fat	0.5 g	Sodium	12.0 mg
Monounsaturated fat	1.0 g	Zinc	1.2 mg
Polyunsaturated fat	2.2 g	**Other Fats**	
Vitamins		Omega-3 fatty acids	0.0 g
A—beta-carotene	2724.8 mcg	Omega-6 fatty acids	0.4 g
Vitamin B6	0.1 mg		
Vitamin C	517.6 mg		

Apricot Creme Topping

This creamy apricot mixture is delicious over hot cereal. My husband and I ate it with hot oatmeal and coconut the day we invented it. The mixture had a slightly butterscotch taste because unsulfured apricots were used. This topping also makes a great-tasting pudding.

Nutrisip: Apricots are rich in beta-carotene, a powerful cancer-fighting antioxidant. Unsulfured apricots are a healthier choice; look for brown-colored dried apricots at your health food store.

8 ounces soft silken tofu
10 dried apricots, soaked (barely cover with water to keep flavor)
1/4 cup hazelnut or almond amazake or 1/4 cup plain soy milk and 2 tablespoons honey plus 1/4 teaspoon pure almond extract
1/2 teaspoon pure vanilla extract
1/2 teaspoon ascorbic acid (vitamin C powder)

Place the tofu, apricots, amazake (or soy milk, honey, and almond extract), vanilla, and ascorbic acid in a blender and blend on high speed until smooth. Serve over hot cereal or chill, covered, until ready to serve. You can also serve as a pudding—chill first in dessert cups. This can be stored, covered, in the refrigerator for one or two days.

Umebushi Plum Tofu Topping

Total Weight:	20.0 oz.	Serving Size:	5.0 oz.

Serves 4

Basic Components

Calories	81.0	Vitamin E	0.2 IU
Calories from fat	21.8	Folate	4.9 mcg
Protein	4.0 g	**Minerals**	
Carbohydrates	12.0 g	Calcium	26.8 mg
Dietary fiber	1.1 g	Iron	0.8 mg
Sugar—total	5.9 g	Magnesium	21.9 mg
Fat—total	2.4 g	Potassium	254.8 mg
Saturated fat	0.3 g	Selenium	0.1 mcg
Monounsaturated fat	0.4 g	Sodium	4.7 mg
Polyunsaturated fat	1.1 g	Zinc	0.4 mg
Vitamins		**Other Fats**	
A—beta-carotene	172.9 mcg	Omega-3 fatty acids	0.0 g
Vitamin B6	0.0 mg	Omega-6 fatty acids	0.0 g
Vitamin C	8.6 mg		

Umebushi Plum Tofu Topping

This is a terrific topping for soups, steamed vegetables, potatoes, or rice; spread it over hot corn bread or use it as a dip.

Nutrisip: The medicinal properties of umebushi (pickled) plums (balancing for excesses) and garlic (natural antibiotic) make this an excellent addition to your diet to help ward off those winter colds and flu bugs or to knock them out of commission at the first symptoms.

1 10-ounce cube soft silken tofu
1/4–1/2 cup parsley, rinsed
4 pickled (umebushi) plums, seeds removed
1 garlic clove, peeled

Combine the tofu, parsley, plums, and garlic in a blender and blend on high speed until smooth. Serve immediately, or store covered in the refrigerator until ready to serve. This will keep in the refrigerator for about one week.

Coffee-Break Shakes and Smoothie Pick-Me-Uppers

Americans consume more than 100 billion cups of coffee a year. We're putting a lot of trust in that Java. But what does it really do for us? A cup of coffee can help increase flagging energy and mental functioning. But too much coffee can cause headaches, tremors, palpitations, insomnia, and indigestion and can raise your blood pressure. It can worsen other conditions, such as osteoporosis; coffee has been linked to decreased bone density, perhaps because it causes a person to excrete calcium. Drinking coffee throughout the day can have a negative impact on cognitive abilities. Coffee elevates levels of stress hormones, which negatively impact the part of the brain that is involved in learning and memory.

Why not take your next coffee break with something healthy—a delicious shake or smoothie? Feed your body nutrients that will have long-lasting positive effects. For example, all fruits and vegetables give us potassium, and some are very rich in this mineral, such as carrots, cantaloupe, tomatoes, and peaches. Potassium plays a key role in energy metabolism in our bodies, and low levels are associated with fatigue and exhaustion. Selenium is a mineral that helps energize the body and relieve fatigue; it's abundant in grapes, oranges, and carrots.

If your job demands a quick, alert mind, you'll want to increase the amount of antioxidants you consume. Free radicals can attack brain cells, contributing to brain aging, but antioxidants such as vitamins C and E, beta-carotene, selenium, various enzymes, and phytonutrients all act as scavengers to keep free radicals from your cells. The recipes in this book are loaded with these nutrients. Whether you want to increase memory, enhance creativity, improve concentration, or boost alertness, dietary boosters from healthy smoothie ingredients can make a terrific difference. For example, choline, which is found in spinach and oranges, can help fight fatigue and improve mental performance, and lecithin, which is a supplement I often add to smoothies, is one of the best sources of choline.

Try the following recipes to make your midmorning and midafternoon breaks the healthiest and best for you by giving your body the right fuel for energy, endurance, and peak performance.

Carob Peanut Butter Banana

Total Weight:	23.1 oz.	Serving Size:	7.7 oz.

Serves 3

Basic Components

Calories	174.7
Calories from fat	67.4
Protein	7.5 g
Carbohydrates	22.8 g
Dietary fiber	3.7 g
Sugar—total	15.6 g
Fat—total	7.5 g
Saturated fat	1.4 g
Monounsaturated fat	2.9 g
Polyunsaturated fat	2.3 g

Vitamins

A—beta-carotene	37.8 mcg
Vitamin B6	0.6 mg
Vitamin C	7.2* mg
Vitamin E	1.9 IU
Folate	29.4 mcg

Minerals

Calcium	26.5 mg
Iron	2.3 mg
Magnesium	56.9 mg
Potassium	509.8 mg
Selenium	2.7 mcg
Sodium	82.0 mg
Zinc	0.7 mg

Other Fats

Omega-3 fatty acids	0.1 g
Omega-6 fatty acids	2.1 g

*Some protein powders contain Vitamin C. Adding the optional Protein powder may increase your Vitamin C count.

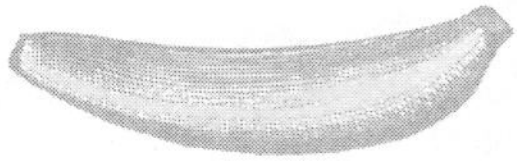

Carob Peanut Butter Banana

Did you ever eat peanut butter and banana sandwiches when you were a kid? Maybe you still do. This shake reminds me of those sandwiches, only it's better. Your kids will love this one, too.

Nutrisip: Carob is a nutritious alternative to chocolate because it is free of stimulants, namely caffeine. And this smoothie is loaded with nutrients to fuel the brain and energize the whole body.

1 cup plain soy milk or milk of choice
2 frozen bananas
2 tablespoons peanut butter, creamy or crunchy
1 tablespoon protein powder (optional)
1/2 teaspoon ascorbic acid (vitamin C powder)
6 ice cubes

Pour the milk into a blender and add the frozen bananas, peanut butter, protein powder as desired, ascorbic acid, and ice cubes. Blend on high speed until smooth and serve immediately.

Peachy Almond Surprise

Total Weight: 26.0 oz. Serving Size: 13.0 oz.

Serves 2

Basic Components

Calories	157.5
Calories from fat	14.8
Protein	1.7 g
Carbohydrates	34.7 g
Dietary fiber	3.7 g
Sugar—total	29.9 g
Fat—total	1.6 g
Saturated fat	0.1 g
Monounsaturated fat	0.9 g
Polyunsaturated fat	0.1 g
Vitamins	
A—beta-carotene	417.2 mcg
Vitamin B6	0.0 mg
Vitamin C	10.4 mg
Vitamin E	9.5 IU
Folate	5.7 mcg
Minerals	
Calcium	112.3 mg
Iron	0.4 mg
Magnesium	13.8 mg
Potassium	392.6 mg
Selenium	0.8 mcg
Sodium	79.1 mg
Zinc	0.3 mg
Other Fats	
Omega-3 fatty acids	0.0 g
Omega-6 fatty acids	0.1 g

Peachy Almond Surprise

This is a beautiful peach-colored drink that is as appealing to the eye as it is to the taste buds.

Nutrisip: Peaches are a good source of beta-carotene, which helps protect the skin from harmful UV rays.

1 cup almond milk (soy milk can be substituted)
2 large or 3 small ripe peaches, peeled, pitted and diced
1–2 tablespoons honey (optional)
1 teaspoon pure vanilla extract
1/2 teaspoon pure almond extract
6 ice cubes

Pour the almond milk into a blender and add the peaches, honey as desired, vanilla and almond extracts, and top with ice. Blend on high speed until smooth.

Spice Swirl

Total Weight:	13.0 oz.	Serving Size:	6.5 oz.

Serves 2

Basic Components

Calories	89.4
Calories from fat	14.2
Protein	2.8 g
Carbohydrates	16.0 g
Dietary fiber	0.2 g
Sugar—total	14.7 g
Fat—total	1.6 g
Saturated fat	0.2 g
Monounsaturated fat	0.3 g
Polyunsaturated fat	0.9 g

Vitamins

A—beta-carotene	1.1 mcg
Vitamin B6	0.0 mg
Vitamin C	0.1 mg
Vitamin E	0.2 IU
Folate	0.1 mcg

Minerals

Calcium	19.8 mg
Iron	0.5 mg
Magnesium	17.3 mg
Potassium	260.1 mg
Selenium	0.0 mcg
Sodium	17.3 mg
Zinc	0.3 mg

Other Fats

Omega-3 fatty acids	0.0 g
Omega-6 fatty acids	0.0 g

Spice Swirl

A delightfully spicy smoothie with a Middle Eastern flavor.

Nutrisip: Cardamom is an aromatic spice used in the Middle East, Latin America, and Asia. It stimulates digestion and eases indigestion.

1 cup apple juice (about two apples, juiced, if making fresh)
1-inch chunk gingerroot (juice with the apples or grate)
4 ounces soft silken tofu (plain yogurt can be substituted)
1/8 teaspoon ground black pepper
1/8 teaspoon ground cumin
1/8 teaspoon ground cardamom

Pour the apple juice and ginger juice (or grated ginger) into a blender and add the tofu, pepper, cumin, and cardamom. Blend on high speed until smooth and serve immediately.

New England Summer Delight

Total Weight: 11.4 oz. Serving Size: 5.7 oz.

Serves 2

Basic Components

Calories	46.6
Calories from fat	1.5
Protein	0.4 g
Carbohydrates	12.0 g
Dietary fiber	1.7 g
Sugar—total	10.0 g
Fat—total	0.2 g
Saturated fat	0.0 g
Monounsaturated fat	0.0 g
Polyunsaturated fat	0.1 g
Vitamins	
A—beta-carotene	33.0 mcg
Vitamin B6	0.0 mg
Vitamin C	5.4 mg
Vitamin E	0.6 IU
Folate	2.9 mcg
Minerals	
Calcium	5.7 mg
Iron	0.1 mg
Magnesium	4.4 mg
Potassium	78.9 mg
Selenium	0.4 mcg
Sodium	5.4 mg
Zinc	0.1 mg
Other Fats	
Omega-3 fatty acids	0.0 g
Omega-6 fatty acids	0.0 g

New England Summer Delight

This smoothie looks and tastes like a blueberry milk shake.

Nutrisip: During World War II, fighter pilots were given bilberry extracts to help improve their night vision. (Bilberry is similiar to the blueberry.) If you're having trouble adjusting from dark to light or seeing as well at night as in daytime, try adding more blueberries to your diet.

1/2 cup unsweetened applesauce
1/2 cup fresh or frozen blueberries, rinsed if fresh
6 mint leaves, rinsed
6 ice cubes

Pour the applesauce into a blender and add the blueberries, mint leaves, and ice cubes. Blend on high speed until smooth and serve immediately.

The Best Way to Rinse Berries

Treating your berries harshly bruises the fruit and causes the loss of some juice. Also, washing them in water that is too warm can cause vital nutrients to slip right down the drain. The best way to rinse fresh berries is to place them in a bowl of cool water and stir them gently with your hand or a wooden spoon. Drain the water and repeat. Dry in a colander. And don't forget, the healthiest berries are grown organically (see pages 8–10 for more information).

Berry Delicious

Total Weight:	16.6 oz.	Serving Size:	8.3 oz.

Serves 2

BASIC COMPONENTS

Calories	267.5
Calories from fat	145.4
Protein	5.7 g
Carbohydrates	28.5 g
Dietary fiber	3.0 g
Sugar—total	17.7 g
Fat—total	16.2 g
Saturated fat	3.2 g
Monounsaturated fat	9.4 g
Polyunsaturated fat	2.8 g

VITAMINS

A—beta-carotene	43.5 mcg
Vitamin B6	0.1 mg
Vitamin C	9.4 mg
Vitamin E	1.4 IU
Folate	28.3 mcg

MINERALS

Calcium	21.1 mg
Iron	2.2 mg
Magnesium	93.3 mg
Potassium	333.8 mg
Selenium	4.4 mcg
Sodium	18.8 mg
Zinc	2.0 mg

OTHER FATS

Omega-3 fatty acids	0.1 g
Omega-6 fatty acids	2.7 g

Berry Delicious

Raw cashews help thicken smoothies and are a good alternative to yogurt or tofu.

Nutrisip: Cashews are rich in magnesium, a mineral that has been shown to help lower blood pressure. Fruits and vegetables in general have shown positive effects in lowering blood pressure.

1/2 cup apple juice (1 apple, juiced)
1 cup fresh or frozen blueberries, rinsed if fresh
1/2 cup unsalted cashews (raw cashews taste best)
1/2 teaspoon pure vanilla extract
6 ice cubes

Pour the apple juice into a blender and add the blueberries, cashews, vanilla, and ice cubes. Blend on high speed until smooth and serve immediately.

Chai Smoothie

Total Weight:	18.2 oz.	Serving Size:	9.1 oz.

Serves 2

BASIC COMPONENTS

Calories	130.2
Calories from fat	24.3
Protein	4.1 g
Carbohydrates	25.5 g
Dietary fiber	3.5 g
Sugar—total	19.5 g
Fat—total	2.7 g
Saturated fat	0.4 g
Monounsaturated fat	0.4 g
Polyunsaturated fat	1.1 g

VITAMINS

A—beta-carotene	30.5 mcg
Vitamin B6	0.4 mg
Vitamin C	5.7 mg
Vitamin E	0.3 IU
Folate	13.6 mcg

MINERALS

Calcium	20.1 mg
Iron	1.2 mg
Magnesium	42.2 mg
Potassium	417.6 mg
Selenium	2.3 mcg
Sodium	18.2 mg
Zinc	0.4 mg

OTHER FATS

Omega-3 fatty acids	0.2 g
Omega-6 fatty acids	0.9 g

Chai Smoothie

If you like chai tea flavor, you'll love this smoothie.

Nutrisip: Used in Chinese, Indian, and Southeast Asian cuisine, coriander helps the digestive system by stimulating the secretion of gastric juices; it also helps reduce flatulence.

1 cup plain soy milk or milk of choice
1 banana, peeled and cut in chunks
1/2 teaspoon ground cinnamon
1/8 teaspoon ground cardamom
1/8 teaspoon ground coriander
1/8 teaspoon ground cloves
1/8 teaspoon ground black pepper
1/8 teaspoon stevia or 1 tablespoon honey
6 ice cubes (or 6 frozen chai tea cubes)

Pour the milk into a blender and add the banana, cinnamon, cardamom, coriander, cloves, black pepper, sweetener, and ice. (As an option, you can pour steeped chai tea into an ice cube tray and add frozen tea cubes to your smoothie.) Blend on high speed until smooth. Serve immediately.

Peachy Morning

Total Weight:	25.0 oz.	Serving Size:	12.5 oz.

Serves 2

BASIC COMPONENTS

Calories	223.3
Calories from fat	34.6
Protein	9.6 g
Carbohydrates	40.0 g
Dietary fiber	4.2 g
Sugar—total	35.0 g
Fat—total	3.8 g
Saturated fat	1.5 g
Monounsaturated fat	0.9 g
Polyunsaturated fat	0.8 g
VITAMINS	
A—beta-carotene	309.9 mcg
Vitamin B6	0.1 mg
Vitamin C	11.7 mg
Vitamin E	1.1 IU
Folate	20.8 mcg
MINERALS	
Calcium	241.9 mg
Iron	0.9 mg
Magnesium	47.2 mg
Potassium	708.1 mg
Selenium	5.7 mcg
Sodium	93.8 mg
Zinc	1.4 mg
OTHER FATS	
Omega-3 fatty acids	0.2 g
Omega-6 fatty acids	0.6 g

Peachy Morning

This smoothie tastes best made with ripe peaches picked in season (peak months are July and August), when they are the sweetest. Toward the end of the season (September and October), they can be somewhat mealy and lack flavor. When not in peak season, it is best to use frozen peaches that have been harvested and frozen during their peak.

Nutrisip: Peaches are a good source of beta-carotene, manganese, potassium, and inositol. Inositol is not considered an essential vitamin; however, one of its many roles is in the body's use of fats and cholesterol. It has been shown to alleviate or prevent the accumulation of excess fat in the liver.

1/2 cup soy milk or milk of choice
1 cup plain low-fat yogurt
1 cup frozen peaches, cut in chunks (if using fresh peaches, cut in chunks and freeze ahead)
1 cup frozen cherries
1 tablespoon honey or to taste
1 teaspoon pure vanilla extract

Pour the milk into a blender and add the yogurt, peaches, cherries, honey to taste, and vanilla. Blend on high speed until smooth and serve immediately.

Tropical Break

Total Weight:	12.1 oz.	Serving Size:	12.1 oz.

Serves 1

Basic Components

Calories	130.6
Calories from fat	33.6
Protein	6.0 g
Carbohydrates	18.9 g
Dietary fiber	5.4 g
Sugar—total	9.5 g
Fat—total	3.7 g
Saturated fat	0.5 g
Monounsaturated fat	0.7 g
Polyunsaturated fat	1.6 g

Vitamins

A—beta-carotene	76.4 mcg
Vitamin B6	0.1 mg
Vitamin C	97.8 mg
Vitamin E	2.6 IU
Folate	60.9 mcg

Minerals

Calcium	47.9 mg
Iron	1.2 mg
Magnesium	50.6 mg
Potassium	654.5 mg
Selenium	3.3 mcg
Sodium	26.9 mg
Zinc	0.5 mg

Other Fats

Omega-3 fatty acids	0.2 g
Omega-6 fatty acids	1.4 g

Tropical Break

Tastes like a Creamsicle or a yummy dessert!

Nutrisip: Papaya contains papain, a protein-digesting enzyme that can help alleviate inflammation and improve digestion.

3/4 cup plain soy milk or milk of choice
1 small papaya, cut in chunks and frozen (about 1 1/2 cups)
1 1/2 teaspoons freshly grated lemon peel, preferably organic
1 teaspoon pure vanilla extract

Pour the milk into a blender and add the papaya, lemon peel, and vanilla. Blend on high speed until smooth and serve immediately.

Mango Madness

Total Weight: 22.6 oz. Serving Size: 11.3 oz.

Serves 2

Basic Components			
Calories	164.3	Vitamin E	3.0 IU
Calories from fat	6.8	Folate	54.1 mcg
Protein	1.8 g	**Minerals**	
Carbohydrates	41.3 g	Calcium	25.6 mg
Dietary fiber	3.5 g	Iron	0.5 mg
Sugar—total	35.7 g	Magnesium	37.8 mg
Fat—total	0.8 g	Potassium	586.3 mg
Saturated fat	0.2 g	Selenium	1.4 mcg
Monounsaturated fat	0.2 g	Sodium	5.7 mg
Polyunsaturated fat	0.1 g	Zinc	0.2 mg
Vitamins		**Other Fats**	
A—beta-carotene	2478.6 mcg	Omega-3 fatty acids	0.1 g
Vitamin B6	0.5 mg	Omega-6 fatty acids	0.1 g
Vitamin C	80.6 mg		

Mango Madness

A tropical treat!

Nutrisip: For your health, choose mangoes grown in the United States or none at all. The U.S. State Department has allowed imported mangoes to be irradiated and/or sprayed with chemicals banned in this country to prevent the spread of mango-seed weevils.

3/4 cup fresh orange juice (2 oranges, juiced) or pineapple juice
1-inch chunk gingerroot, juiced or grated
1 ripe medium mango, peeled and cut into chunks from the pit
1 banana, peeled and cut in chunks
6 ice cubes

Pour the orange or pineapple juice and ginger juice or grated ginger in a blender and add the mango, banana, and ice. Blend on high speed until smooth and serve immediately.

Figgy's Banana

Total Weight:	26.2 oz.	Serving Size:	13.1 oz.

Serves 2

Basic Components

Calories	265.0	Vitamin E	2.0 IU
Calories from fat	82.3	Folate	29.6 mcg
Protein	6.9 g	**Minerals**	
Carbohydrates	43.6 g	Calcium	58.4 mg
Dietary fiber	7.5 g	Iron	2.1 mg
Sugar—total	31.2 g	Magnesium	95.8 mg
Fat—total	9.2 g	Potassium	759.4 mg
Saturated fat	1.8 g	Selenium	4.5 mcg
Monounsaturated fat	4.0 g	Sodium	20.3 mg
Polyunsaturated fat	2.3 g	Zinc	1.3 mg
Vitamins		**Other Fats**	
A—beta-carotene	129.5 mcg	Omega-3 fatty acids	0.2 g
Vitamin B6	0.6 mg	Omega-6 fatty acids	2.1 g
Vitamin C	507.8 mg		

Figgy's Banana

An unusually delicious blend of flavors!

Nutrisip: Figs are a good source of calcium, iron, magnesium, and potassium. Combine them with calcium-rich cashews and soy milk and you have a terrific bone-strengthening smoothie.

1 cup plain soy milk or milk of choice
6 fresh ripe small black figs, cut in half
1 medium frozen banana, cut in chunks
*3 tablespoons raw cashews, roasted**
1 teaspoon pure vanilla extract
1/2 teaspoon ground nutmeg
1/2 teaspoon ascorbic acid (vitamin C powder)
4–6 ice cubes (optional)

Pour the soy milk into a blender and add the figs, banana, cashews, vanilla, nutmeg, ascorbic acid, and ice cubes as desired. Blend until smooth and serve immediately.

**Roast cashews in a 350° F. oven for 10–15 minutes, or until golden brown.*

Plum Peachy

Total Weight: 22.8 oz. Serving Size: 11.4 oz.

Serves 2

Basic Components

Calories	144.1
Calories from fat	16.9
Protein	3.3 g
Carbohydrates	31.1 g
Dietary fiber	4.6 g
Sugar—total	23.8 g
Fat—total	1.9 g
Saturated fat	0.3 g
Monounsaturated fat	0.5 g
Polyunsaturated fat	0.7 g
Vitamins	
A—beta-carotene	346.0 mcg
Vitamin B6	0.4 mg
Vitamin C	16.0 mg
Vitamin E	1.6 IU
Folate	16.1 mcg
Minerals	
Calcium	13.5 mg
Iron	0.7 mg
Magnesium	38.9 mg
Potassium	572.4 mg
Selenium	2.0 mcg
Sodium	9.9 mg
Zinc	0.4 mg
Other Fats	
Omega-3 fatty acids	0.1 g
Omega-6 fatty acids	0.6 g

Plum Peachy

If you're looking for a terrific midmorning or midafternoon flavor boost, this is a delicious blend of fruit. You may not think of plums when you think of smoothies, yet they add great flavor.

Nutrisip: Plums are a good source of bioflavonoids, a class of compounds that act as powerful antioxidants, which protect the body against free-radical damage.

1/2 cup soy milk or milk of choice
1 teaspoon pure vanilla extract
4 small ripe purple plums, rinsed, seeded, and cut in half
1 large peach, peeled, seeded, and chopped into 1- to 2-inch chunks
1 frozen banana, cut into chunks
6 ice cubes

Pour the milk into a blender and add the vanilla, plums, peach, banana, and ice. Blend on high speed until smooth and serve immediately.

Hazelnut Dream

Total Weight:	19.8 oz.	Serving Size:	9.9 oz.

Serves 2

BASIC COMPONENTS			
Calories	297.6	Vitamin E	6.8 IU
Calories from fat	180.9	Folate	45.6 mcg
Protein	8.4 g	MINERALS	
Carbohydrates	26.4 g	Calcium	44.4 mg
Dietary fiber	6.3 g	Iron	2.5 mg
Sugar—total	12.5 g	Magnesium	88.2 mg
Fat—total	20.1 g	Potassium	608.1 mg
Saturated fat	1.7 g	Selenium	3.5 mcg
Monounsaturated fat	13.6 g	Sodium	23.4 mg
Polyunsaturated fat	3.4 g	Zinc	1.1 mg
VITAMINS		OTHER FATS	
A—beta-carotene	35.2 mcg	Omega-3 fatty acids	0.2 g
Vitamin B6	0.6 mg	Omega-6 fatty acids	3.2 g
Vitamin C	7.2 mg		

Hazelnut Dream

Amazake is a naturally sweet rice drink that can be found at most health food or whole food stores; almond amazake can be substituted.

Nutrisip: Hazelnuts are a good source of calcium and magnesium, as are almonds. Magnesium works with enzymes in the body to break down glucose stored in the liver to create energy. And energy is what you need from that midmorning or midday pick-me-upper!

1 cup hazelnut or almond amazake (or substitute 1 cup milk of choice and 1/2 cup nuts)*
1 frozen banana, cut in chunks
1 tablespoon carob powder (optional)
6 ice cubes

Pour the amazake (or milk and nuts) into a blender and add the banana, carob powder as desired, and ice cubes. Blend on high speed until smooth and serve immediately.

**If you can't find amazake in your area, make this smoothie with 1 cup soy or rice milk and 1/2 cup hazelnuts or almonds.*

Grandma's Rhubarb Smoothie

Total Weight: 26.4 oz. Serving Size: 13.2 oz.

Serves 2

Basic Components

Calories	224.3
Calories from fat	23.3
Protein	7.3 g
Carbohydrates	47.7 g
Dietary fiber	5.1 g
Sugar—total	38.0 g
Fat—total	2.6 g
Saturated fat	0.9 g
Monounsaturated fat	0.5 g
Polyunsaturated fat	0.7 g
Vitamins	
A—beta-carotene	83.7 mcg
Vitamin B6	0.2 mg
Vitamin C	11.7 mg
Vitamin E	0.8 IU
Folate	18.0 mcg
Minerals	
Calcium	260.6 mg
Iron	1.9 mg
Magnesium	52.4 mg
Potassium	878.3 mg
Selenium	4.5 mcg
Sodium	62.7 mg
Zinc	1.4 mg
Other Fats	
Omega-3 fatty acids	0.1 g
Omega-6 fatty acids	0.6 g

Grandma's Rhubarb Smoothie

This is a sweet-tart smoothie. It reminds me of the rhubarb raisin pie my grandmother made with rhubarb she grew in her garden.

Nutrisip: Rhubarb is high in oxalates, binders that combine chemically with calcium and other minerals to prevent their absorption. It is interesting to note, however, that rhubarb itself is fairly high in calcium, 348 mg per 1 cup cooked rhubarb.

1/2 cup plain soy milk
1 cup Stewed Rhubarb and Raisins (see page 74 for recipe)
1/2 cup plain low-fat yogurt
1 teaspoon natural cinnamon extract or cinnamon powder
1/8 teaspoon stevia or sweetener of choice to taste
6 ice cubes

Pour the soy milk into a blender and add the rhubarb raisin mixture, yogurt, cinnamon, sweetener, and ice cubes. Blend until smooth and serve immediately.

Terrific Health-and-Healing Smoothies

Are you eating between five and nine servings of fruits and vegetables every day? This is the number recommended by the federal government to maintain good health. If you're like most Americans, the answer is no. Surveys show that only one in eleven people eats even the minimum of five servings daily. Many people are so busy that preparation of these vital foods seems to take a backseat to everything else. Don't despair if this is you—smoothies can revolutionize your life. They take only minutes to make, and you can load them up with fresh fruits and vegetables—yes, even vegetables—and make them delicious.

If you're faced with a health challenge, it's even more important to incorporate plenty of fresh fruits, and *especially vegetables,* into your diet. These foods offer increased energy and stamina and strengthened immunity, plus the raw materials your body needs to heal itself more quickly and completely. If you want to prevent disease, the best path to a disease-free life of vitality begins with a diet rich in plant foods. Smoothies are a delicious, simple way of increasing your consumption of these life-giving foods.

In this chapter I've addressed some common health complaints with smoothie recipes that offer specific foods or nutrients which have been shown to help that condition. For example, Bone-Up Solution (page 123) offers nutrients that support strong bones to help you prevent osteoporosis. Cold Stomper (page 129), Flu Terminator (page 145), and Immune Booster (page 133) may become some of your best allies during cold and flu season, because what you eat can help you speed your recovery or prolong your illness. Cranberry Infection Fighter (page 147) incorporates the famous little cranberry that has been shown in scientific studies to heal bladder infections. And for those occasions of excess, whether it be too much stress, too much travel, or too much alcohol, you can find relief with the Stress Buster (page 157), Jet-Lag Soother (page 153), or Hangover Helper (page 143).

Curb Your Cravings

Total Weight:	17.6 oz.	Serving Size:	8.8 oz.

Serves 2

BASIC COMPONENTS

Calories	121.2
Calories from fat	38.3
Protein	3.0 g
Carbohydrates	20.5 g
Dietary fiber	2.3 g
Sugar—total	14.4 g
Fat—total	4.3 g
Saturated fat	0.7 g
Monounsaturated fat	1.5 g
Polyunsaturated fat	1.8 g
VITAMINS	
A—beta-carotene	43.3 mcg
Vitamin B6	0.4 mg
Vitamin C	25.0 mg
Vitamin E	0.5 IU
Folate	18.6 mcg
MINERALS	
Calcium	26.0 mg
Iron	0.6 mg
Magnesium	24.9 mg
Potassium	636.5 mg
Selenium	0.8 mcg
Sodium	76.7 mg
Zinc	0.5 mg
OTHER FATS	
Omega-3 fatty acids	0.0 g
Omega-6 fatty acids	0.0 g

Curb Your Cravings

This is one of my favorite smoothies. It has an unusual blend of ingredients that combine into fabulous flavor.

Nutrisip: This smoothie is loaded with vitamin E, chromium, and vanadium—all nutrients that help curb cravings, especially for carbohydrates.

1/2 apple, washed and juiced (about 1/4 cup juice)
1/2 cup spinach, washed and juiced
1 celery stalk, washed and juiced
1 tablespoon tahini (sesame butter)
1 banana, peeled and cut in chunks
6 ice cubes

Pour the apple, spinach, and celery juices into a blender and add the tahini, banana, and ice. Blend on high speed until smooth and serve immediately.

Cherie's No-Sugar Smoothie

Total Weight:	14.1 oz.	Serving Size:	14.1 oz.

Serves 1

Basic Components			
Calories	288.6	Vitamin C	4.0 mg
Calories from fat	146.6	Vitamin E	1.0 IU
Protein	15.5 g	Folate	42.4 mcg
Carbohydrates	20.9 g	**Minerals**	
Dietary fiber	0.8 g	Calcium	472.7 mg
Sugar—total	17.4 g	Iron	0.9 mg
Fat—total	16.3 g	Magnesium	58.5 mg
Saturated fat	4.2 g	Potassium	643.8 mg
Monounsaturated fat	4.5 g	Selenium	8.4 mcg
Polyunsaturated fat	5.7 g	Sodium	181.2 mg
Cholesterol	15.0 mg	Zinc	2.9 mg
Vitamins		**Other Fats**	
A—beta-carotene	2.5 mcg	Omega-3 fatty acids	0.3 g
Vitamin B6	0.1 mg	Omega-6 fatty acids	1.9 g

Cherie's No-Sugar Smoothie

This is not a sweet smoothie, as the name reflects, but it is packed with flavor, which makes up for the lack of fruit sugars. You can add stevia, an herbal sweetener that can be metabolized well by people with sugar metabolism challenges.

Nutrisip: This sugar-free smoothie is for everyone who has a sugar metabolism problem or anyone who wants to cut back on carbohydrates. If you are prone to low blood sugar (hypoglycemic), as I am, or are diabetic, I think you'll appreciate the blend of ingredients that makes this smoothie flavorful without fruit or honey.

1 cup plain low-fat yogurt
1 tablespoon tahini (sesame butter)
1 teaspoon pure raspberry extract
1 teaspoon pure vanilla extract
1 teaspoon lecithin granules
1/2 teaspoon freshly grated orange peel, preferably organic
1/4 teaspoon stevia (optional)
6 ice cubes

Place the yogurt, tahini, raspberry extract, vanilla, lecithin, orange peel, stevia as desired, and ice in a blender and process on high speed until smooth. Serve immediately.

Bone-Up Solution

Total Weight: 25.6 oz. Serving Size: 12.8 oz.

Serves 2

BASIC COMPONENTS

Calories	184.1	Vitamin E	0.3 IU
Calories from fat	16.1	Folate	21.0 mcg
Protein	3.0 g	MINERALS	
Carbohydrates	43.7 g	Calcium	16.3 mg
Dietary fiber	3.3 g	Iron	0.8 mg
Sugar—total	27.2 g	Magnesium	37.3 mg
Fat—total	1.8 g	Potassium	487.6 mg
Saturated fat	0.2 g	Selenium	1.6 mcg
Monounsaturated fat	0.2 g	Sodium	15.6 mg
Polyunsaturated fat	0.6 g	Zinc	0.4 mg
VITAMINS		OTHER FATS	
A—beta-carotene	75.5 mcg	Omega-3 fatty acids	0.1 g
Vitamin B6	0.4 mg	Omega-6 fatty acids	0.5 g
Vitamin C	46.6 mg		

Bone-Up Solution

It's good for your bones, but your taste buds will love this smoothie, too.

Nutrisip: Deep blue-red berries such as blueberries, blackberries, and raspberries are rich in anthocyanidins and proanthocyanidins. These are the flavonoids that stabilize collagen structure. This is significant information because collagen is the major protein structure of the bones and adds elasticity to the skin. These ingredients make an excellent bone-strengthening smoothie.

1/2 cup apple juice (1 apple juiced)
Juice of 1/2 lemon, peel removed if using a juice machine
1/2 cup plain soy milk or milk of choice
1 cup fresh or frozen blueberries, blackberries, or raspberries, rinsed if fresh
1/8 teaspoon stevia or 1 tablespoon honey (optional)
1 banana, peeled and cut into chunks
6 ice cubes

Pour the apple and lemon juices and soy milk into a blender and add the berries, sweetener as desired, banana, and ice. Blend on high speed until smooth and serve immediately.

You Won't Get a Lemon!

Did you know that the white part of the citrus just under the skin contains the most vitamin C and bioflavonoids—phytochemicals that help your body absorb and store more precious, immune-boosting vitamin C? That's right! When you start with a tangy lemon, you can blend it with other tasty ingredients and get the fabulous nutritional benefits. Organic is best. And a lemon will increase the nutritional benefits of any smoothie.

Tummy Soother

Total Weight:	16.4 oz.	Serving Size:	8.2 oz.

Serves 2

BASIC COMPONENTS

Calories	184.1	Vitamin E	0.6 IU
Calories from fat	46.3	Folate	6.6 mcg
Protein	5.0 g	MINERALS	
Carbohydrates	30.0 g	Calcium	293.4 mg
Dietary fiber	11.9 g	Iron	6.4 mg
Sugar—total	14.7 g	Magnesium	7.6 mg
Fat—total	5.1 g	Potassium	558.4 mg
Saturated fat	0.0 g	Selenium	1.0 mcg
Monounsaturated fat	0.1 g	Sodium	30.6 mg
Polyunsaturated fat	0.1 g	Zinc	0.1 mg
VITAMINS		OTHER FATS	
A—beta-carotene	86.1 mcg	Omega-3 fatty acids	0.0 g
Vitamin B6	0.0 mg	Omega-6 fatty acids	0.1 g
Vitamin C	4.3 mg		

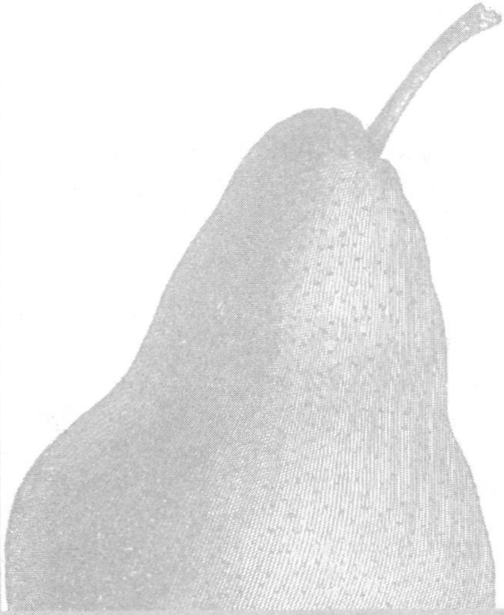

Tummy Soother

This is one of the most delicious smoothies I've ever conceived, but it tastes even better as a frozen dessert. See Anise Ice (page 311).

Nutrisip: Fennel has been used since ancient times for soothing digestion. Mint and anise have also been long-used remedies for indigestion. Pear and applesauce are known to be soothing for the stomach.

1/2 cup fresh fennel juice (3–4 stalks fennel)
1/2 cup unsweetened applesauce
1/2 teaspoon pure anise extract
6 mint leaves, rinsed
1 ripe pear, washed, stem removed, and cut into chunks
6 ice cubes

Pour the fennel juice into a blender and add the applesauce, anise, mint, pear, and ice cubes. Blend on high speed until smooth and serve immediately.

Better-Than-Chicken-Soup Souper Smoothie

Total Weight: 24.4 oz. Serving Size: 6.1 oz.

Serves 4

Basic Components

Calories	151.4
Calories from fat	80.9
Protein	3.7 g
Carbohydrates	16.1 g
Dietary fiber	4.2 g
Sugar—total	6.9 g
Fat—total	9.0 g
Saturated fat	1.7 g
Monounsaturated fat	1.7 g
Polyunsaturated fat	5.1 g
Vitamins	
A—beta-carotene	158.1 mcg
Vitamin B6	0.2 mg
Vitamin C	10.2 mg
Vitamin E	0.5 IU
Folate	23.3 mcg
Minerals	
Calcium	103.2 mg
Iron	1.1 mg
Magnesium	42.6 mg
Potassium	456.0 mg
Selenium	2.3 mcg
Sodium	317.4 mg
Zinc	0.6 mg
Other Fats	
Omega-3 fatty acids	3.8 g
Omega-6 fatty acids	1.2 g

Better-Than-Chicken-Soup Souper Smoothie

This fine-restaurant style cold soup can be made with leftover squash from the night before or you could bake an extra squash when you prepare dinner. The soup can be prepared ahead of time and stored in the refrigerator. It will thicken as it sits; you may want to add a little soy milk to thin it to desired consistency.

Nutrisip: If you're feeling ill and you need a boost to your immune system, this soup is loaded with immune enhancers and helpers. Onions and garlic have antibacterial properties, squash is loaded with beta-carotene, which is superfood for the immune cells and the adrenal glands, clove is antiseptic, and cinnamon has been used as a medicine to treat colds since ancient times. If you're feeling cold, you can gently warm this soup on low heat.

1 cup onion, chopped
2 garlic cloves, minced
1 teaspoon butter or oil
1/2 cup plain soy milk
1 cup peeled, cooked, and mashed squash (choose any sweet winter squash, such as acorn, butternut, or turban)
1/2 cup plain low-fat yogurt
1 teaspoon ground cinnamon
1/2 teaspoon sea salt
1/4 teaspoon ground cloves
2 tablespoons pure cold-pressed flaxseed oil

Sauté the onion and garlic in butter or oil for about 10 minutes on low heat, or until the onion is transparent. Pour the soy milk into the blender and add the onion mixture, squash, yogurt, cinnamon, salt, and cloves. Blend on high speed until smooth. While the blender is running, drizzle in the flaxseed oil slowly.

Cold Stomper

Total Weight:	16.9 oz.	Serving Size:	16.9 oz.

Serves 1

BASIC COMPONENTS

Calories	203.8
Calories from fat	8.7
Protein	3.9 g
Carbohydrates	50.0 g
Dietary fiber	10.6 g
Sugar—total	37.6 g
Fat—total	1.0 g
Saturated fat	0.1 g
Monounsaturated fat	0.1 g
Polyunsaturated fat	0.4 g

VITAMINS

A—beta-carotene	7153.0 mcg
Vitamin B6	0.2 mg
Vitamin C	214.0 mg
Vitamin E	3.5 IU
Folate	46.6 mcg

MINERALS

Calcium	87.3 mg
Iron	0.9 mg
Magnesium	66.6 mg
Potassium	1115.9 mg
Selenium	2.8 mcg
Sodium	48.0 mg
Zinc	0.4 mg

OTHER FATS

Omega-3 fatty acids	0.1 g
Omega-6 fatty acids	0.4 g

Cold Stomper

This smoothie has a very tart flavor because of the grapefruit, but if you're home with a cold, your immune system will thank you for drinking it. Cut off as much of the white part of the grapefruit as possible if you want to reduce the bitterness of the juice, but be aware that you will get fewer nutrients.

Nutrisip: Grapefruit is loaded with vitamin C and bioflavonoids, especially in the white pithy part—supernutrients for the immune cells. Carrot is rich in beta-carotene, another immune cell superfood. Fresh gingerroot is used in Chinese medicine for treating colds, and cayenne pepper acts as a decongestant and expectorant. This should chase a cold away!

1 grapefruit, peeled and juiced
1 carrot, green top removed, ends trimmed, scrubbed, and juiced
1-inch chunk gingerroot, juiced
2 kiwifruit, peeled and cut in half
Dash of cayenne pepper (optional)

Pour the grapefruit, carrot, and ginger juices into a blender and add kiwi; blend on high speed. Add a dash of cayenne pepper as desired, stir, and serve immediately.

Delicious Digestion

Total Weight:	18.8 oz.	Serving Size:	9.4 oz.

Serves 2

Basic Components

Calories	110.8
Calories from fat	6.6
Protein	1.2 g
Carbohydrates	27.5 g
Dietary fiber	3.6 g
Sugar—total	20.6 g
Fat—total	0.7 g
Saturated fat	0.0 g
Monounsaturated fat	0.1 g
Polyunsaturated fat	0.1 g
Vitamins	
A—beta-carotene	35.0 mcg
Vitamin B6	0.1 mg
Vitamin C	63.7 mg
Vitamin E	0.8 IU
Folate	14.1 mcg
Minerals	
Calcium	33.7 mg
Iron	0.6 mg
Magnesium	14.4 mg
Potassium	351.5 mg
Selenium	1.1 mcg
Sodium	2.6 mg
Zinc	0.2 mg
Other Fats	
Omega-3 fatty acids	0.0 g
Omega-6 fatty acids	0.1 g

Delicious Digestion

This is a light, mint-flavored shake that's low calorie, too.

Nutrisip: Grapes are rich in bioflavonoids, plant chemicals that increase vitamin C absorption to a greater extent. Pears are rich in pectin, soluble fiber that promotes good colon health. Kiwifruit are fairly good sources of vitamin C, and mint is rich in flavonoids, which stimulate the liver and gallbladder, increasing the flow of bile.

1/2 cup white grape juice (1 cup green grapes, juiced)
1 pear, washed, stem removed, and cut into chunks
1 kiwifruit, peeled and cut in half
6 mint leaves, rinsed
6 ice cubes

Pour the grape juice into a blender and add the pear, kiwi, mint, and ice. Blend on high speed until smooth and serve immediately.

Immune Booster

Total Weight:	23.4 oz.	Serving Size:	11.7 oz.

Serves 2

Basic Components

Calories	306.0	Vitamin E	0.7 IU
Calories from fat	99.5	Folate	29.6 mcg
Protein	5.9 g	**Minerals**	
Carbohydrates	47.9 g	Calcium	53.5 mg
Dietary fiber	2.9 g	Iron	2.1 mg
Sugar—total	21.9 g	Magnesium	72.8 mg
Fat—total	11.1 g	Potassium	567.2 mg
Saturated fat	2.2 g	Selenium	3.5 mcg
Monounsaturated fat	6.3 g	Sodium	54.9 mg
Polyunsaturated fat	2.0 g	Zinc	1.6 mg
Vitamins		**Other Fats**	
A—beta-carotene	13232.1 mcg	Omega-3 fatty acids	0.1 g
Vitamin B6	0.3 mg	Omega-6 fatty acids	1.9 g
Vitamin C	38.3 mg		

Immune Booster

This is a great way to use leftover sweet potatoes.

Nutrisip: If you're feeling a bit "under the weather," this smoothie could help you on your way to feeling better more quickly with a wallop of beta-carotene for your immune system from the carrot juice and sweet potato, the pineapple's bromelain (an enzyme with anti-inflammatory compounds), and the anti-inflammatory properties and high zinc content of gingerroot. If you have a bronchial condition, omit the ice; it's taxing to the respiratory system.

1/2 cup fresh carrot juice (3–5 carrots, juiced)
1/2 cup fresh pineapple juice (1/4 pineapple, juiced)
1- to 2-inch chunk gingerroot, juiced
3/4 cup cooked sweet potato, skin removed, mashed
1/3 cup raw cashews
6 ice cubes (optional)

Pour the carrot, pineapple, and ginger juices into a blender and add the sweet potato, cashews, and ice cubes as desired. Blend on high speed until smooth, and serve immediately.

Souper Recovery

Total Weight:	50.0 oz.	Serving Size:	12.5 oz.

Serves 4

BASIC COMPONENTS

Calories	285.5
Calories from fat	55.7
Protein	9.6 g
Carbohydrates	50.7 g
Dietary fiber	6.5 g
Sugar—total	4.3 g
Fat—total	6.2 g
Saturated fat	0.7 g
Monounsaturated fat	1.1 g
Polyunsaturated fat	3.5 g

VITAMINS

A—beta-carotene	707.0 mcg
Vitamin B6	0.8 mg
Vitamin C	71.2 mg
Vitamin E	1.0 IU
Folate	65.0 mcg

MINERALS

Calcium	67.3 mg
Iron	4.2 mg
Magnesium	88.6 mg
Potassium	1685.5 mg
Selenium	2.5 mcg
Sodium	475.0 mg
Zinc	1.6 mg

OTHER FATS

Omega-3 fatty acids	2.0 g
Omega-6 fatty acids	1.5 g

Souper Recovery

You can gently warm this mixture, if you want something warmly soothing. Keep the heat low, and don't let the soup get too hot. This way you'll preserve more of the vitamins and enzymes. If you do warm this soup, add the flax oil after heating to preserve the essential fatty acids.

Nutrisip: Parsley is one of nature's best sources of vitamin C, ounce for ounce about triple that of the orange. It's also very rich in bioflavonoids, which greatly enhance vitamin C absorption. Flaxseed oil helps to regulate the immune system. And garlic is a natural antibiotic. I'll bet you're feeling better already, just reading this.

6 new white potatoes, cubed, with skins (about 3 1/2 cups)
1 cup purified water
8 garlic cloves, roasted
2 cups plain soy milk
1 1/2 cups parsley, coarsely chopped
1/2–1 teaspoon sea salt, or to taste
1/2 teaspoon dried tarragon
1 tablespoon pure cold-pressed flaxseed oil

Cook the potatoes in 1 cup of water for 30 minutes or until soft. Roast the garlic (see page 281 for instructions). Cool the potatoes in the refrigerator until cold. Pour the soy milk into a blender and add the garlic, potatoes, parsley, salt, and tarragon. Blend on high speed until smooth. Keep the blender running while you slowly drizzle the flaxseed oil into the mixture. Serve immediately or store in the refrigerator until ready to serve.

Colon Care

Total Weight: 15.6 oz. Serving Size: 7.8 oz.

Serves 2

Basic Components

Calories	187.4
Calories from fat	51.6
Protein	9.8 g
Carbohydrates	27.3 g
Dietary fiber	5.4 g
Sugar—total	16.1 g
Fat—total	5.7 g
Saturated fat	1.6 g
Monounsaturated fat	1.4 g
Polyunsaturated fat	2.4 g
Vitamins	
A—beta-carotene	182.3 mcg
Vitamin B6	0.2 mg
Vitamin C	2.0 mg
Vitamin E	1.3 IU
Folate	44.7 mcg
Minerals	
Calcium	270.2 mg
Iron	1.9 mg
Magnesium	79.1 mg
Potassium	516.5 mg
Selenium	7.6 mcg
Sodium	92.5 mg
Zinc	1.8 mg
Other Fats	
Omega-3 fatty acids	1.8 g
Omega-6 fatty acids	0.6 g

Colon Care

You'll be surprised at how good this smoothie tastes. Honest.

Nutrisip: Prunes and oat bran really do promote good colon regularity; studies have proved it. Add to that the fiber of flaxseed, and you can drink your way to a healthy colon.

1 cup plain low-fat yogurt
2 tablespoons oat bran
2 tablespoons flaxseed
1 teaspoon ground cinnamon
1 teaspoon pure vanilla extract
4 prunes, soaked in water first if hard
6 ice cubes

Combine the yogurt, oat bran, flaxseed, cinnamon, vanilla, prunes, and ice in a blender and blend on high speed until smooth. Serve immediately.

Tropical Enzyme Delight

Total Weight:	12.6 oz.	Serving Size:	12.6 oz.

Serves 1

BASIC COMPONENTS

Calories	176.6
Calories from fat	39.9
Protein	9.4 g
Carbohydrates	25.3 g
Dietary fiber	6.5 g
Sugar—total	9.5 g
Fat—total	4.4 g
Saturated fat	1.0 g
Monounsaturated fat	0.7 g
Polyunsaturated fat	1.7 g

VITAMINS

A—beta-carotene	83.1 mcg
Vitamin B6	0.2 mg
Vitamin C	105.1 mg
Vitamin E	4.3 IU
Folate	61.4 mcg

MINERALS

Calcium	60.2 mg
Iron	2.1 mg
Magnesium	58.2 mg
Potassium	687.6 mg
Selenium	3.3 mcg
Sodium	27.5 mg
Zinc	1.3 mg

OTHER FATS

Omega-3 fatty acids	0.2 g
Omega-6 fatty acids	1.4 g

Tropical Enzyme Delight

Tastes like an orange Creamsicle!

Nutrisip: Bee pollen contains enzymes along with the orange and papaya—the papaya being rich in papain, a protein-digesting enzyme. The body also manufactures enzymes, but people who do not eat raw foods or supplement with enzymes put a great strain on their bodies because cooked food is devoid of enzymes; they are killed during the heating process.

1 small papaya, peeled, seeds removed, cut in chunks (about 1 1/2 cups)
3/4 cup plain soy milk or milk of choice
1 1/2 teaspoons freshly grated orange peel, preferably organic
1 teaspoon pure vanilla extract
1 teaspoon bee pollen

Place the papaya chunks in a freezer bag and freeze them until solid. Pour the soy milk into a blender and add the papaya, orange peel, vanilla, and bee pollen. Blend on high speed until smooth and serve immediately.

Arabian Nights and Sweet Dreams

Total Weight: 15.8 oz. Serving Size: 7.9 oz.

Serves 2

BASIC COMPONENTS

Calories	237.3
Calories from fat	146.2
Protein	5.3 g
Carbohydrates	22.7 g
Dietary fiber	3.9 g
Sugar—total	14.3 g
Fat—total	16.2 g
Saturated fat	2.4 g
Monounsaturated fat	4.0 g
Polyunsaturated fat	7.1 g

VITAMINS

A—beta-carotene	43.8 mcg
Vitamin B6	0.4 mg
Vitamin C	28.1 mg
Vitamin E	1.4 IU
Folate	39.1 mcg

MINERALS

Calcium	44.4 mg
Iron	1.3 mg
Magnesium	47.3 mg
Potassium	454.3 mg
Selenium	2.0 mcg
Sodium	14.9 mg
Zinc	1.0 mg

OTHER FATS

Omega-3 fatty acids	0.4 g
Omega-6 fatty acids	3.2 g

Arabian Nights and Sweet Dreams

This smoothie has a thin, juicy consistency, with a rich, exotic flavor.

Nutrisip: A deficiency of calcium and/or magnesium can cause you to wake up in the middle of the night and not be able to fall back to sleep. Soy, sesame, and orange are good sources of calcium; soy and banana are rich in magnesium. A deficiency of copper or iron is believed to contribute to insomnia. Soy lecithin is rich in copper and sesame and banana are good sources of iron.

1/2 cup plain soy milk or milk of choice
2 tablespoons tahini (sesame butter)
1 1/2 teaspoons freshly grated orange peel, preferably organic
1 tablespoon soy lecithin granules
1 teaspoon pure vanilla extract
1 banana, peeled and cut in chunks
1/2 orange, peeled and cut in chunks
4 ice cubes

Pour the milk into a blender and add the tahini, orange peel, lecithin, vanilla, banana, orange chunks, and ice. Blend on high speed until smooth and serve immediately.

Hangover Helper

Total Weight: 28.8 oz. Serving Size: 14.4 oz.

Serves 2

Basic Components

Calories	147.1
Calories from fat	66.4
Protein	2.4 g
Carbohydrates	21.8 g
Dietary fiber	2.6 g
Sugar—total	13.7 g
Fat—total	7.4 g
Saturated fat	0.7 g
Monounsaturated fat	1.5 g
Polyunsaturated fat	4.9 g
Vitamins	
A—beta-carotene	1354.7 mcg
Vitamin B6	0.3 mg
Vitamin C	1055.9 mg
Vitamin E	3.3 IU
Folate	41.7 mcg
Minerals	
Calcium	38.4 mg
Iron	1.1 mg
Magnesium	27.1 mg
Potassium	681.5 mg
Selenium	1.3 mcg
Sodium	51.1 mg
Zinc	0.4 mg
Other Fats	
Omega-3 fatty acids	3.8 g
Omega-6 fatty acids	1.1 g

Hangover Helper

Not only does this smoothie soothe your hangover, it tastes good to boot.

Nutrisip: The liver is quite adversely impacted by overconsumption of alcohol. Tomato juice and lemon juice will help to revitalize it and improve vitality. Japanese pickled plums (also known as umebushi plums) are used in macrobiotic medicine to counteract the effects of overconsumption of alcohol. Alcohol also is very dehydrating; drink several glasses of water in addition to drinking this smoothie.

1 1/2 cups fresh tomato juice (about 3 tomatoes, juiced)
1/2 cup fresh carrot juice (3 medium carrots, juiced)
1/2 lemon, juiced, and peeled if using a juice machine
1 tablespoon pure cold-pressed flaxseed oil (optional)
1 teaspoon ascorbic acid (vitamin C powder)
2 pickled (umebushi) plums, seeds removed
6 ice cubes

Pour the tomato, carrot, and lemon juices into a blender and add the flaxseed oil, ascorbic acid, pickled plums, and ice. Blend on high speed until smooth and serve immediately.

Pickled plums or umebushi plums, as they are sometimes called, are medicinal Japanese plums that taste salty and sour. They are packed with shiso leaves, which can also be eaten. Macrobiotic practitioners use them for hangovers because they are *yang* (meaning salty and contracted), and they are considered effective for counteracting the effects of too much alcohol or sugar (*yin*). They are used for colds and flu, too, because these conditions are also conditions of excess. Pickled plums can be found in the Oriental or macrobiotic section of health food stores, whole food markets, or Asian markets. Always remove the seeds before blending them in a recipe.

Flu Terminator

Total Weight:	15.6 oz.	Serving Size:	7.8 oz.

Serves 2

Basic Components

Calories	59.6
Calories from fat	5.9
Protein	1.8 g
Carbohydrates	14.4 g
Dietary fiber	2.4 g
Sugar—total	8.3 g
Fat—total	0.7 g
Saturated fat	0.1 g
Monounsaturated fat	0.2 g
Polyunsaturated fat	0.2 g
Vitamins	
A—beta-carotene	543.0 mcg
Vitamin B6	0.2 mg
Vitamin C	45.8 mg
Vitamin E	1.1 IU
Folate	28.9 mcg
Minerals	
Calcium	23.9 mg
Iron	0.7 mg
Magnesium	20.4 mg
Potassium	465.8 mg
Selenium	1.1 mcg
Sodium	32.7 mg
Zinc	0.2 mg
Other Fats	
Omega-3 fatty acids	0.0 g
Omega-6 fatty acids	0.2 g

Flu Terminator

Ice is omitted from this smoothie because ice-cold drinks are too taxing for digestive and respiratory systems already weakened by a virus. For speedier recovery, it is best to drink beverages close to room temperature.

Nutrisip: This smoothie is rich in vitamins C and E, beta-carotene, selenium, and zinc—nutrients that strengthen the immune system to fight the infection. In addition, garlic has antibiotic properties. And Japanese pickled plums are used in macrobiotic medicine for colds and flu, which are conditions of excess.

2 radishes, scrubbed and juiced
1 stalk celery, juiced
1/2 lemon, juiced, peeled if using a juice machine
2 cups tomatoes, rinsed and chopped (about 2 tomatoes)
1 garlic clove, peeled
1–2 pickled (umebushi) plums, seeds removed
1/2 teaspoon freshly grated lemon peel, preferably organic
Dash of cayenne pepper

Pour the radishes, celery and the lemon juices into a blender and add the tomatoes, garlic, plums, lemon peel, and cayenne. Blend on high speed until smooth and serve immediately.

Cranberry Infection Fighter

Total Weight:	15.2 oz.	Serving Size:	7.6 oz.

Serves 2

Basic Components

Calories	68.5	Vitamin E	0.0 IU
Calories from fat	0.5	Folate	0.5 mcg
Protein	0.1 g	**Minerals**	
Carbohydrates	17.2 g	Calcium	3.2 mg
Dietary fiber	1.0 g	Iron	0.1 mg
Sugar—total	16.0 g	Magnesium	2.4 mg
Fat—total	0.1 g	Potassium	173.6 mg
Saturated fat	0.0 g	Selenium	0.2 mcg
Monounsaturated fat	0.0 g	Sodium	16.3 mg
Polyunsaturated fat	0.0 g	Zinc	0.1 mg
Vitamins		**Other Fats**	
A—beta-carotene	7.0 mcg	Omega-3 fatty acids	0.0 g
Vitamin B6	0.0 mg	Omega-6 fatty acids	0.0 g
Vitamin C	3.3 mg		

Cranberry Infection Fighter

This is a delicious cranberry juice combination that is much healthier for you than commercial cranberry cocktail, which has added sugars and additives. Dried cranberries won't work for this drink, with the exception of a brand called Just Cranberries, which has no sugar and is dried with a special process that keeps the cranberries at their original size. They are made by Just Tomatoes. Though I did not test it, you might try one-half teaspoon of pure cranberry concentrate, found at health food stores, if you can't find any cranberries. If you do not have a juice machine to make your own fresh apple juice, and are using a commercial brand, buy unsweetened; grate the gingerroot.

Nutrisip: Studies have shown that cranberry juice is very helpful in healing and preventing bladder infections. It works by preventing the bacteria from adhering to the bladder wall. Also, gingerroot is an excellent source of zinc, which is a potent infection fighter. Adding vitamin C strengthens your immune system.

1 cup apple juice (2 apples, juiced)
1-inch chunk gingerroot, juiced or grated
1/2 cup fresh or frozen cranberries or Just Cranberries
1/4 teaspoon ascorbic acid (vitamin C powder)
6 ice cubes

Pour the apple juice and ginger juice or grated ginger into a blender and add the cranberries, ascorbic acid, and ice. Blend on high speed until smooth and serve immediately.

Anti-Aging Smoother

Total Weight:	16.4 oz.	Serving Size:	16.4 oz.

Serves 1

BASIC COMPONENTS			
Calories	151.0	Vitamin E	3.6 IU
Calories from fat	6.5	Folate	95.4 mcg
Protein	2.2 g	MINERALS	
Carbohydrates	36.9 g	Calcium	54.2 mg
Dietary fiber	4.7 g	Iron	0.5 mg
Sugar—total	29.2 g	Magnesium	32.5 mg
Fat—total	0.7 g	Potassium	672.3 mg
Saturated fat	0.1 g	Selenium	1.4 mcg
Monounsaturated fat	0.1 g	Sodium	13.6 mg
Polyunsaturated fat	0.2 g	Zinc	0.3 mg
VITAMINS		OTHER FATS	
A—beta-carotene	159.2 mcg	Omega-3 fatty acids	0.1 g
Vitamin B6	0.1 mg	Omega-6 fatty acids	0.1 g
Vitamin C	407.9 mg		

Anti-Aging Smoother

Save the papaya peel to rub on your face. Papaya makes a great facial because of the enzyme papain, which is a protein-digesting enzyme that helps eliminate dead skin cells.

Nutrisip: Antioxidants are among your best allies in preventing aging because they bind free radicals and carry them out of your system; they would otherwise damage your cells and contribute to the aging process. This smoothie is rich in antioxidants that include vitamins C and E, beta-carotene, selenium, enzymes, and phytonutrients.

1/2 cup orange juice (1–2 oranges, juiced)
1 cup papaya, peeled, seeded, and chopped into chunks
1/2 cup frozen or fresh blueberries
1/4 teaspoon ascorbic acid (vitamin C powder)
*3 ice cubes**

Pour the orange juice into a blender and add the papaya, blueberries, ascorbic acid, and ice. Blend on high speed until smooth and serve immediately.

**If you use fresh blueberries, add 3 additional ice cubes.*

Scrumptious Almond Potassium Shake

Total Weight: 9.8 oz. Serving Size: 4.9 oz.

Serves 2

Basic Components

Calories	181.9
Calories from fat	89.8
Protein	4.5 g
Carbohydrates	19.5 g
Dietary fiber	3.9 g
Sugar—total	13.7 g
Fat—total	10.0 g
Saturated fat	0.8 g
Monounsaturated fat	6.1 g
Polyunsaturated fat	2.1 g
Vitamins	
A—beta-carotene	28.3 mcg
Vitamin B6	0.4 mg
Vitamin C	5.4 mg
Vitamin E	10.2 IU
Folate	19.1 mcg
Minerals	
Calcium	54.6 mg
Iron	0.3 mg
Magnesium	18.0 mg
Potassium	271.1 mg
Selenium	0.7 mcg
Sodium	38.9 mg
Zinc	0.1 mg
Other Fats	
Omega-3 fatty acids	0.0 g
Omega-6 fatty acids	2.1 g

Scrumptious Almond Potassium Shake

A luscious, creamy shake with an almond flavor.

Nutrisip: Bananas and almonds are excellent sources of potassium; almonds are the highest. Surprised? If you're prone to leg or foot cramps, you may be potassium deficient. Also, potassium deficiency has been linked with high blood pressure.

1/2 cup almond milk or milk of choice
1/4 cup raw almonds
1/2 teaspoon pure almond extract
1 frozen banana, cut in chunks

Pour the milk into a blender and add the almonds, almond extract, and banana. Blend on high speed until smooth. Serve immediately.

Jet-Lag Soother

Total Weight:	11.9 oz.	Serving Size:	5.9 oz.

Serves 2

BASIC COMPONENTS

Calories	30.3
Calories from fat	0.4
Protein	1.4 g
Carbohydrates	7.7 g
Dietary fiber	1.7 g
Sugar—total	3.7 g
Fat—total	0.0 g
Saturated fat	0.0 g
Monounsaturated fat	0.0 g
Polyunsaturated fat	0.0 g
VITAMINS	
A—beta-carotene	147.1 mcg
Vitamin B6	0.1 mg
Vitamin C	527.5 mg
Vitamin E	0.2 IU
Folate	14.5 mcg
MINERALS	
Calcium	34.6 mg
Iron	0.5 mg
Magnesium	5.5 mg
Potassium	302.0 mg
Selenium	0.4 mcg
Sodium	23.7 mg
Zinc	0.1 mg
OTHER FATS	
Omega-3 fatty acids	0.0 g
Omega-6 fatty acids	0.0 g

Jet-Lag Soother

This is one of my favorite morning juice drinks. I turned it into a smoothie by freezing the cucumber.

Nutrisip: Traveling across time zones is very stressful to the body and especially to the adrenal glands. If you are a frequent traveler, it is very important that you support your adrenal glands with ample organic sodium (celery and cucumber), vitamin C (lemon), and especially pantothenic acid (nutritional yeast is the best source).

1/2 cucumber, peeled and cut in chunks
1 stalk celery, juiced or chopped into small pieces
1/2 lemon, juiced, peeled if using a juice machine
1/2 teaspoon freshly grated lemon peel, preferably organic
1/2 teaspoon ascorbic acid (vitamin C powder)
Sprinkle of nutritional yeast as desired

Place the cucumber chunks in a freezer bag and freeze them until solid. Combine the cucumber chunks in a blender with the celery, lemon juice, lemon peel, and ascorbic acid. Blend on high speed until smooth, sprinkle with nutritional yeast as desired, and serve immediately.

Wild Berry Bright Eyes

Total Weight:	14.6 oz.	Serving Size:	7.3 oz.

Serves 2

Basic Components

Calories	82.5
Calories from fat	13.1
Protein	2.2 g
Carbohydrates	16.8 g
Dietary fiber	3.2 g
Sugar—total	8.4 g
Fat—total	1.5 g
Saturated fat	0.1 g
Monounsaturated fat	0.2 g
Polyunsaturated fat	0.6 g

Vitamins

A—beta-carotene	39.0 mcg
Vitamin B6	0.1 mg
Vitamin C	12.3 mg
Vitamin E	0.4 IU
Folate	16.0 mcg

Minerals

Calcium	18.0 mg
Iron	0.7 mg
Magnesium	21.5 mg
Potassium	198.9 mg
Selenium	1.1 mcg
Sodium	10.5 mg
Zinc	0.3 mg

Other Fats

Omega-3 fatty acids	0.1 g
Omega-6 fatty acids	0.5 g

Wild Berry Bright Eyes

A creamy, colorful berry smoothie!

Nutrisip: Berries are rich in antioxidants that help fight degenerative eye disorders and also help improve vision. Also to help prevent eye disorders, avoid sugar—it promotes swelling of the lens and increases the risk of free-radical damage to the eyes.

6 Wild Berry Zinger herbal tea ice cubes
1/2 cup soy milk or milk of choice
1/2 cup blackberries, washed
1/2 cup blueberries, washed
2 teaspoons honey
1/4 teaspoon pure raspberry extract

Steep one bag of Wild Berry Zinger herbal tea in a cup of hot water for about 20 minutes, or until the tea is strong and flavorful. Pour the tea into six ice cube tray squares and freeze until solid. Pour the milk into a blender and add the berries, honey, raspberry extract, and Wild Berry Zinger tea ice cubes. Blend on high speed until smooth and serve immediately.

Stress Buster

Total Weight: 19.2 oz. Serving Size: 9.6 oz.

Serves 2

BASIC COMPONENTS

Calories	82.1
Calories from fat	1.5
Protein	1.0 g
Carbohydrates	19.9 g
Dietary fiber	1.7 g
Sugar—total	13.5 g
Fat—total	0.2 g
Saturated fat	0.0 g
Monounsaturated fat	0.0 g
Polyunsaturated fat	0.1 g

VITAMINS

A—beta-carotene	875.1 mcg
Vitamin B6	0.0 mg
Vitamin C	22.8 mg
Vitamin E	0.9 IU
Folate	3.3 mcg

MINERALS

Calcium	21.5 mg
Iron	0.2 mg
Magnesium	6.6 mg
Potassium	380.2 mg
Selenium	0.3 mcg
Sodium	33.9 mg
Zinc	0.2 mg

OTHER FATS

Omega-3 fatty acids	0.0 g
Omega-6 fatty acids	0.1 g

Stress Buster

Delicious and light.

Nutrisip: Carrots are a good source of magnesium (needed during times of stress), potassium (needs increase with stress to support adrenal glands), and selenium (protects against infections). Chamomile is helpful for insomnia, anxiety, and digestive problems stemming from a nervous condition.

6 chamomile herbal tea ice cubes
1/2 cup pineapple juice (about 1/4 pineapple, juiced)
1/2 cup fresh carrot juice (3–5 carrots, juiced)
1 cup fresh or frozen peaches, sliced

Steep one chamomile herbal tea bag in a cup of hot water for about 20 minutes or until the tea is strong and flavorful. Pour the tea into six ice cube tray squares and freeze. Pour the pineapple and carrot juices into a blender and add the peaches and chamomile tea ice cubes. Blend on high speed until smooth and serve immediately.

Workout and Bodybuilding Smoothies

To increase your energy for workouts and bodybuilding, pay particular attention to the fuel reserves in the muscles and to the muscles' ability to use that fuel. Vitamins, minerals, enzymes, phytonutrients, and water are all vital parts of that process. The best way to put nutrients into your body is with a balanced diet and especially with high-quality foods such as the smoothies in this section. Smoothies, like fresh juices, are broken down into easily absorbed nutrients that your body can assimilate and absorb quickly.

Also, be aware that during intense training or competition sports, body temperature increases, making you sweat. This causes the viscosity and salt concentration of the blood to rise, along with the heart rate. Blood sugar levels change and often drop too low. Many experts agree that when you lose 1 percent of your body fluid, your performance is reduced by 10 percent. Therefore, it is important to replace fluids as you work out, along with valuable nutrients such as electrolytes, to help maintain proper blood volume and blood sugar levels. See Competition Gator Shake (page 169) for an excellent fluid/nutrient replacer that has no artificial ingredients or concentrated sugars—just pure juices, natural sweetener, and nutrients.

When you work out, the natural metabolic processes can generate molecules known as *free radicals.* These are unpaired electrons looking to steal an electron from another cell, thereby damaging it. Antioxidants such as vitamins C and E, beta-carotene, selenium, and certain enzymes and phytonutrients all act as scavengers of free radicals. Antioxidants can be particularly helpful when it comes to sore muscles, especially for the weekend athlete or individuals who exercise vigorously. Occasional exercise can result in delayed-onset muscle soreness that is due to microscopic tears in the muscle; antioxidants can help prevent or heal such tears. Antioxidants also help control free-radical and lipid peroxidation that naturally occurs with the rise in oxygen consumption associated with exercise. Fresh fruits and vegetables are loaded with antioxidants along with many of the other smoothie ingredients used in my recipes.

Healthy Start

Total Weight: 14.0 oz. Serving Size: 14.0 oz.

Serves 1

BASIC COMPONENTS

Calories	257.5
Calories from fat	141.6
Protein	7.5 g
Carbohydrates	24.9 g
Dietary fiber	2.3 g
Sugar—total	20.6 g
Fat—total	15.7 g
Saturated fat	3.4 g
Monounsaturated fat	2.0 g
Polyunsaturated fat	6.3 g
VITAMINS	
A—beta-carotene	17.1 mcg
Vitamin B6	0.1 mg
Vitamin C	504.2 mg
Vitamin E	1.6 IU
Folate	14.5 mcg
MINERALS	
Calcium	243.1 mg
Iron	0.6 mg
Magnesium	28.2 mg
Potassium	385.8 mg
Selenium	4.4 mcg
Sodium	92.6 mg
Zinc	1.4 mg
OTHER FATS	
Omega-3 fatty acids	0.7 g
Omega-6 fatty acids	5.5 g

Healthy Start

This smoothie makes a great breakfast-in-a-glass before a morning workout. It offers lots of nutrients without a lot of bulk, so you won't have a too-full feeling before you exercise.

Nutrisip: Unsweetened applesauce is a great addition to any smoothie because it adds thickness without fat and sweetness and flavor without a lot of sugar. Apples are low on the glycemic index, meaning they are low in fruit sugars, making them a good choice for people with sugar metabolism challenges, such as hypoglycemia and diabetes, and good for everyone because they are high in pectin, soluble fiber that helps regulate blood sugar.

1/2 cup unsweetened applesauce
1/2 cup plain low-fat yogurt
1 tablespoon lecithin granules
1 teaspoon pure vanilla extract
1 teaspoon bee pollen
1/2 teaspoon pure cinnamon extract or ground cinnamon
1/2 teaspoon ascorbic acid (vitamin C powder)
6 ice cubes

Pour the applesauce into a blender and add the yogurt, lecithin, vanilla, bee pollen, cinnamon, ascorbic acid, and ice. Blend on high until smooth and serve immediately.

Muscle Power Plus

Total Weight:	19.4 oz.	Serving Size:	9.7 oz.

Serves 2

Basic Components

Calories	245.4	Vitamin E	3.2 IU
Calories from fat	116.7	Folate	37.6 mcg
Protein	10.4 g	**Minerals**	
Carbohydrates	25.0 g	Calcium	43.6 mg
Dietary fiber	4.7 g	Iron	1.8 mg
Sugar—total	16.0 g	Magnesium	90.4 mg
Fat—total	13.0 g	Potassium	580.4 mg
Saturated fat	2.3 g	Selenium	2.9 mcg
Monounsaturated fat	4.8 g	Sodium	89.5 mg
Polyunsaturated fat	4.9 g	Zinc	1.3 mg
Vitamins		**Other Fats**	
A—beta-carotene	28.3 mcg	Omega-3 fatty acids	1.0 g
Vitamin B6	0.5 mg	Omega-6 fatty acids	2.9 g
Vitamin C	505.5 mg		

Muscle Power Plus

A good high-protein vegan smoothie. Even if you're a carnivore, you'll love this drink.

Nutrisip: Wheat germ and bananas are high in chromium, which aids in the breakdown and distribution of protein and carbohydrates so the body can use those fuels efficiently. Chromium can also help increase muscle mass faster. Wheat germ, peanuts, soy, and bananas are rich in magnesium—an important mineral in strength training, specifically helpful in torque gain.

1/2 cup soy milk
1/2 cup soft silken tofu
2 tablespoons peanut butter, creamy or crunchy
1 tablespoon flaxseed
1 teaspoon honey
1 teaspoon pure vanilla extract
1 teaspoon wheat germ
1/2 teaspoon ascorbic acid (vitamin C powder)
1 banana, peeled and cut into chunks
6 ice cubes

Pour the soy milk into a blender and add the tofu, peanut butter, flaxseed, honey, vanilla, wheat germ, ascorbic acid, banana, and ice. Blend on high speed until smooth and serve immediately.

Orange Power-Up

Total Weight:	23.0 oz.	Serving Size:	11.5 oz.

Serves 2

BASIC COMPONENTS

Calories	143.5	Vitamin E	0.5 IU
Calories from fat	14.2	Folate	59.4 mcg
Protein	3.7 g	MINERALS	
Carbohydrates	31.3 g	Calcium	63.3 mg
Dietary fiber	5.6 g	Iron	0.7 mg
Sugar—total	24.0 g	Magnesium	43.4 mg
Fat—total	1.6 g	Potassium	569.2 mg
Saturated fat	0.3 g	Selenium	2.7 mcg
Monounsaturated fat	0.3 g	Sodium	11.3 mg
Polyunsaturated fat	0.6 g	Zinc	0.3 mg
VITAMINS		OTHER FATS	
A—beta-carotene	75.2 mcg	Omega-3 fatty acids	0.1 g
Vitamin B6	0.5 mg	Omega-6 fatty acids	0.5 g
Vitamin C	585.6 mg		

Orange Power-Up

A terrific smoothie for any workout day.

Nutrisip: The need for vitamin B6 increases with a higher turnover of muscle cells; soy and bananas are good sources. Vitamin C protects against exercise-induced damage to the muscles.

1/2 cup soy milk
1 teaspoon pure vanilla extract
1/2 teaspoon ascorbic acid (vitamin C powder)
2 oranges, peeled and cut into chunks
1 banana, peeled and cut into chunks
6 ice cubes

Possible Power-Up Additions

Protein powder
Bee pollen
Spirulena
Flaxseed
Lecithin granules

Pour the soy milk and vanilla into a blender and add the ascorbic acid, oranges, banana, and ice. Add any other power-up ingredients you desire and blend on high speed until smooth. Serve immediately.

High-Power Workout

Total Weight: 13.8 oz. Serving Size: 13.8 oz.

Serves 1

BASIC COMPONENTS

Calories	588.1
Calories from fat	315.2
Protein	23.2 g
Carbohydrates	52.2 g
Dietary fiber	6.6 g
Sugar—total	30.5 g
Fat—total	35.0 g
Saturated fat	5.2 g
Monounsaturated fat	12.7 g
Polyunsaturated fat	14.5 g
VITAMINS	
A—beta-carotene	28.3 mcg
Vitamin B6	0.9 mg
Vitamin C	5.5 mg
Vitamin E	1.1 IU
Folate	70.9 mcg
MINERALS	
Calcium	111.8 mg
Iron	12.0 mg
Magnesium	160.2 mg
Potassium	854.2 mg
Selenium	8.0 mcg
Sodium	158.2 mg
Zinc	3.4 mg
OTHER FATS	
Omega-3 fatty acids	7.8 g
Omega-6 fatty acids	6.3 g

High-Power Workout

This is a low-carbohydrate, high-protein drink, and without the honey it is even lower in carbohydrates. UDO's Choice Beyond Greens is a super blend of ground seeds, greens, herbs, and more. (See page 65 for more info on UDO's greens.)

Nutrisip: Soy and bananas are very good sources of potassium, an electrolyte that is essential for stimulating nerve impulses, maintaining acid-base balance, and converting blood glucose to glycogen (the body's fuel). It also helps to widen blood vessels during a workout, thus increasing blood flow to carry away heat. A deficiency of potassium can cause muscle weakness, problems with muscle contraction, and fatigue.

1 cup soy milk or milk of choice
1/4 cup raw cashews
2 tablespoons protein powder
1 tablespoon pure cold-pressed flaxseed oil
*1 teaspoon spirulena**
*1 teaspoon UDO's Choice Beyond Greens or your favorite green powder**
1/2 teaspoon ascorbic acid (vitamin C powder)
1/8 teaspoon stevia or 1 tablespoon honey
1 frozen banana, cut in chunks

Pour the soy milk into a blender and add the cashews, protein powder, flaxseed oil, spirulena, green powder, ascorbic acid, sweetener, and banana. Blend on high speed until smooth and serve immediately.

**Analysis does not include spirulena or green powder.*

Competition Gator Shake

Total Weight:	22.0 oz.	Serving Size:	11.0 oz.

Serves 2

Basic Components

Calories	111.7
Calories from fat	1.4
Protein	0.8 g
Carbohydrates	30.2 g
Dietary fiber	0.5 g
Sugar—total	24.8 g
Fat—total	0.2 g
Saturated fat	0.0 g
Monounsaturated fat	0.0 g
Polyunsaturated fat	0.0 g

Vitamins

A—beta-carotene	32.1 mcg
Vitamin B6	0.1 mg
Vitamin C	568.1 mg
Vitamin E	0.2 IU
Folate	29.4 mcg

Minerals

Calcium	16.5 mg
Iron	0.2 mg
Magnesium	13.4 mg
Potassium	314.5 mg
Selenium	0.3 mcg
Sodium	299.2 mg
Zinc	0.1 mg

Other Fats

Omega-3 fatty acids	0.0 g
Omega-6 fatty acids	0.0 g

Competition Gator Shake

You can dilute this recipe with water to taste. I recommend up to an equal part water to juice. Diluted, it tastes almost like a commercial sports drink, only better.

Nutrisip: This is an antioxidant-rich electrolyte replacer that is free of artificial ingredients, sugars, and other undesirable additives and has not undergone pasteurization, which kills off nutrients. Talk about a competition edge!

1/2 cup orange juice (2 oranges, juiced, peeled if using a juice machine)
1/2 cup apple juice (1 apple, juiced)
1 lemon, juiced, peeled if using a juice machine
1 lime, juiced, peeled if using a juice machine
1/2 teaspoon ascorbic acid (vitamin C powder)
1/4 teaspoon sea salt
1/8 teaspoon stevia or 1 tablespoon honey
8 ice cubes

Pour the orange, apple, lemon, and lime juices into a blender and add the ascorbic acid, sea salt, sweetener, and ice. Blend on high speed until smooth. Serve immediately, store in the refrigerator, or transport in a thermos.

Carbo Power Pack

Total Weight:	20.3 oz.	Serving Size:	10.1 oz.

Serves 2

BASIC COMPONENTS

Calories	171.4	Vitamin E	2.2 IU
Calories from fat	32.1	Folate	14.4 mcg
Protein	4.3 g	**MINERALS**	
Carbohydrates	31.1 g	Calcium	120.5 mg
Dietary fiber	3.7 g	Iron	0.3 mg
Sugar—total	27.1 g	Magnesium	20.3 mg
Fat—total	3.6 g	Potassium	450.9 mg
Saturated fat	1.0 g	Selenium	2.8 mcg
Monounsaturated fat	0.6 g	Sodium	54.4 mg
Polyunsaturated fat	1.2 g	Zinc	0.7 mg
VITAMINS		**OTHER FATS**	
A—beta-carotene	269.3 mcg	Omega-3 fatty acids	0.2 g
Vitamin B6	0.1 mg	Omega-6 fatty acids	1.0 g
Vitamin C	515.5 mg		

Carbo Power Pack

A yummy smoothie for any sports day.

Nutrisip: If you're doing any kind of competition or endurance sport that lasts more than 90 minutes, you need to increase your carbohydrates. Carbohydrates are good fuel for working muscles. This smoothie can be a delicious part of your carbohydrate intake along with complex carbohydrates from whole grains, legumes, and vegetables.

1/2 cup apple juice (1 apple, juiced)
1/2 cup plain low-fat yogurt
1 cup fresh or frozen blueberries, rinsed if fresh
1 cup frozen unsweetened peaches, sliced
1 teaspoon pure vanilla extract
1 teaspoon soy lecithin granules
1/2 teaspoon ascorbic acid (vitamin C powder)
1/2 teaspoon pure almond extract

Pour the apple juice into a blender and add the yogurt, blueberries, peaches, vanilla, lecithin, ascorbic acid, and almond extract. Blend on high speed until smooth and serve immediately.

Pineapple Super Kick

Total Weight: 30.2 oz. Serving Size: 15.1 oz.

Serves 2

BASIC COMPONENTS

Calories	338.9
Calories from fat	146.9
Protein	9.8 g
Carbohydrates	38.6 g
Dietary fiber	1.8 g
Sugar—total	27.7 g
Fat—total	16.3 g
Saturated fat	2.1 g
Monounsaturated fat	2.4 g
Polyunsaturated fat	9.2 g

VITAMINS

A—beta-carotene	78.8 mcg
Vitamin B6	0.3 mg
Vitamin C	558.8 mg
Vitamin E	1.5 IU
Folate	24.2 mcg

MINERALS

Calcium	72.7 mg
Iron	5.3 mg
Magnesium	38.0 mg
Potassium	496.0 mg
Selenium	0.5 mcg
Sodium	75.1 mg
Zinc	1.0 mg

OTHER FATS

Omega-3 fatty acids	4.2 g
Omega-6 fatty acids	3.7 g

Pineapple Super Kick

With all these supernutrient additions, you'd think this smoothie might taste strange, but it's delicious.

Nutrisip: Zinc is needed for energy metabolism, enzyme production, and wound healing. Low zinc levels could result in reduced endurance capacity, and zinc deficiency is related to muscle fatigue. Gingerroot and soy lecithin are excellent sources of zinc.

1 1/2 cups pineapple juice (about 2/3 ripe pineapple, juiced)
1-inch chunk gingerroot, juiced or grated
1 cup chopped pineapple
5 ounces soft silken tofu
2 tablespoons protein powder
1 tablespoon soy lecithin
2 teaspoons bee pollen
1 teaspoon spirulena
1/2 teaspoon ascorbic acid (vitamin C powder)
1 tablespoon pure cold-pressed flaxseed oil
1 teaspoon pure vanilla extract
6 ice cubes

Pour the pineapple juice and ginger juice or grated ginger into a blender and add the pineapple chunks, tofu, protein powder, lecithin, bee pollen, spirulena, ascorbic acid, flaxseed oil, vanilla, and ice cubes. Blend on high speed until smooth and serve immediately.

For ease in making smoothies, measure the dry ingredients before the wet ingredients; you can then use the same measuring spoons without having to wash them in between.

Super-Punch Peachy Creme

Total Weight: 15.2 oz. Serving Size: 7.6 oz.

Serves 2

Basic Components

Calories	91.3
Calories from fat	9.3
Protein	3.8 g
Carbohydrates	16.9 g
Dietary fiber	1.7 g
Sugar—total	14.6 g
Fat—total	1.0 g
Saturated fat	0.6 g
Monounsaturated fat	0.3 g
Polyunsaturated fat	0.1 g

Vitamins

A—beta-carotene	225.8 mcg
Vitamin B6	0.1 mg
Vitamin C	6.1 mg
Vitamin E	0.9 IU
Folate	10.2 mcg

Minerals

Calcium	117.6 mg
Iron	0.2 mg
Magnesium	17.4 mg
Potassium	318.2 mg
Selenium	2.4 mcg
Sodium	43.8 mg
Zinc	0.7 mg

Other Fats

Omega-3 fatty acids	0.0 g
Omega-6 fatty acids	0.1 g

Super-Punch Peachy Creme

This peachy smoothie makes a terrific after-workout refresher.

Nutrisip: Peaches provide a superhelping of beta-carotene, which can gobble up those exercise-induced free radicals so they don't damage your cells.

6 peach herbal tea ice cubes
1/2 cup plain low-fat yogurt
1 teaspoon honey
1 teaspoon pure vanilla extract
1 cup peaches, peeled, pitted, and sliced (about 1 peach)

Steep one peach herbal tea bag in a cup of hot water for about 20 minutes or until the tea is strong and flavorful. Pour the tea into six ice cube tray squares and freeze. Combine the yogurt in a blender with the honey, vanilla, peaches, and peach ice cubes. Blend on high speed until smooth and serve immediately.

Fountain of Youth

Total Weight: 20.2 oz. Serving Size: 10.1 oz.

Serves 2

Basic Components

Calories	145.0
Calories from fat	19.4
Protein	3.6 g
Carbohydrates	29.5 g
Dietary fiber	2.8 g
Sugar—total	21.2 g
Fat—total	2.2 g
Saturated fat	0.3 g
Monounsaturated fat	0.4 g
Polyunsaturated fat	1.1 g
Vitamins	
A—beta-carotene	49.0 mcg
Vitamin B6	0.2 mg
Vitamin C	23.9 mg
Vitamin E	0.9 IU
Folate	12.4 mcg
Minerals	
Calcium	32.4 mg
Iron	0.8 mg
Magnesium	32.5 mg
Potassium	418.5 mg
Selenium	1.2 mcg
Sodium	7.3 mg
Zinc	0.5 mg
Other Fats	
Omega-3 fatty acids	0.0 g
Omega-6 fatty acids	0.1 g

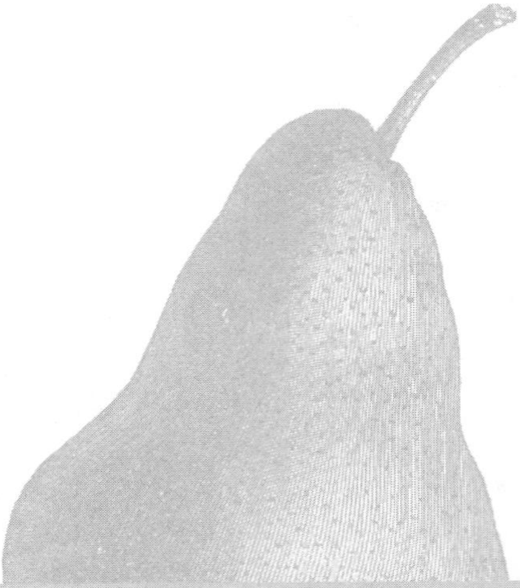

Fountain of Youth

Here's a toast to a younger-looking you.

Nutrisip: Research indicates that higher amounts of sucrose may speed up the aging process. Satisfy your sweet tooth with natural sugars from fresh fruits that are loaded with age-defying antioxidants.

1/2 cup pineapple juice (about 1/4 ripe pineapple, juiced)
1 tablespoon fresh lime juice
1/2 cup soft silken tofu
1 cup fresh pear, washed, stem removed, and sliced (about 1 pear)
1/2 teaspoon freshly grated lime peel, preferably organic
1/2 frozen banana, cut in chunks
4 ice cubes

Pour the pineapple and lime juices into a blender and add the tofu, pear, lime peel, banana, and ice. Blend on high speed until smooth and serve immediately.

Mighty Muscle Mix

Total Weight:	19.4 oz.	Serving Size:	9.7 oz.

Serves 2

Basic Components

Calories	245.4
Calories from fat	116.7
Protein	10.4 g
Carbohydrates	25.0 g
Dietary fiber	4.7 g
Sugar—total	16.0 g
Fat—total	13.0 g
Saturated fat	2.3 g
Monounsaturated fat	4.8 g
Polyunsaturated fat	4.8 g
Vitamins	
A—beta-carotene	28.3 mcg
Vitamin B6	0.5 mg
Vitamin C	505.5 mg
Vitamin E	3.2 IU
Folate	37.6 mcg
Minerals	
Calcium	43.6 mg
Iron	1.8 mg
Magnesium	90.4 mg
Potassium	580.4 mg
Selenium	2.9 mcg
Sodium	89.5 mg
Zinc	1.3 mg
Other Fats	
Omega-3 fatty acids	1.0 g
Omega-6 fatty acids	2.9 g

Mighty Muscle Mix

A creamy and delicious smoothie.

Nutrisip: Cashews add creamy richness without animal fat. And they're high in magnesium, which plays a critical role in converting carbohydrates to energy. Magnesium is needed for cells to make ATP, the molecules that contain energy for the body. This mineral also controls heartbeat and muscle contractions, and it is important for muscle relaxation and prevention of muscle spasms.

2/3 cup apple juice (about 2 apples, juiced)
1 cup fresh or frozen strawberries, washed, caps removed, and sliced if fresh (8–10 strawberries)
1/2 cup raw cashews
1 tablespoon protein powder
1/2 teaspoon ascorbic acid (vitamin C powder)
6 ice cubes

Pour the apple juice into a blender and add the strawberries, cashews, protein powder, ascorbic acid, and ice. Blend on high speed until smooth and serve immediately.

The Athlete's Super Edge

Total Weight: 17.3 oz. Serving Size: 17.3 oz.

Serves 1

Basic Components

Calories	553.4
Calories from fat	332.8
Protein	21.6 g
Carbohydrates	33.8 g
Dietary fiber	10.2 g
Sugar—total	19.3 g
Fat—total	37.0 g
Saturated fat	3.8 g
Monounsaturated fat	22.7 g
Polyunsaturated fat	7.8 g

Vitamins

A—beta-carotene	27.1 mcg
Vitamin B6	0.2 mg
Vitamin C	95.1 mg
Vitamin E	20.7 IU
Folate	69.7 mcg

Minerals

Calcium	420.2 mg
Iron	3.3 mg
Magnesium	245.0 mg
Potassium	988.2 mg
Selenium	5.2 mcg
Sodium	99.0 mg
Zinc	3.7 mg

Other Fats

Omega-3 fatty acids	0.2 g
Omega-6 fatty acids	7.6 g

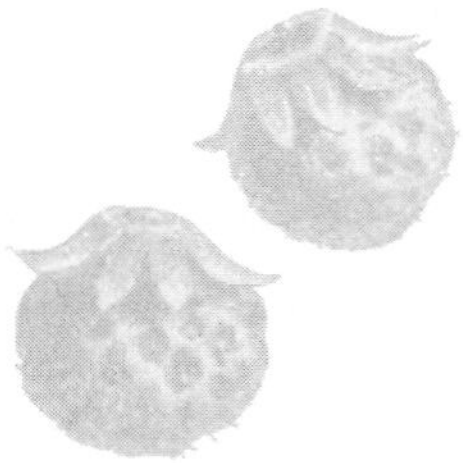

The Athlete's Super Edge

A hint of almond makes this nutritious smoothie exotic as well as delicious.

Nutrisip: Almonds, yogurt, and strawberries are good sources of calcium; even bananas provide a bit of this mineral, which is so important for an athlete. Calcium helps prevent muscle cramps by avoiding lactic acid buildup. And it is also vital for the steady, rhythmic functioning of the cardiovascular system.

1 cup fresh or frozen strawberries, washed and caps removed, if fresh
1/2 cup plain low-fat yogurt
1/2 cup unsalted almonds
1 teaspoon pure vanilla extract
3–4 drops pure almond extract
6 ice cubes
Dash of nutmeg

Combine the strawberries, yogurt, almonds, vanilla, and almond extract in a blender with the ice. Blend on high speed until smooth and add the nutmeg. Serve immediately.

No-Fat Weight-Loss Helpers

The very best way to lose weight is to get the most nutrients for the least amount of calories. It's like choosing the highest rate of return for your investment money without risk. To reach your weight-loss goals, you need to burn more calories than you take in. Eat smart, make your calories count for energy (empty calories are quite likely to get stored as fat), and get more exercise. Low-calorie smoothies and shakes can help you shed those unwanted pounds more quickly, because they are filling and chock-full of nutrients that help you curb cravings.

There are some specific ingredients that you can add to smoothies and shakes that will facilitate weight loss. For example, cucumber, watermelon, parsley, lemon, kiwifruit, and cantaloupe (with seeds) are all natural diuretics that will help you get rid of stored-up water. Though not in this section, the Jet-Lag Soother (page 153) incorporates lemon and cucumber and is deliciously low in calories. Gingerroot has thermogenic properties, meaning that it can help facilitate energy production, which can promote weight loss; see Spicy Tropical Squeeze (page 201). Radishes may help stimulate the thyroid, and healthy thyroid functioning is a key to weight loss and maintenance; try Icy Spicy Tomato (page 189). Daikon radish (a large white radish) has been used in traditional Oriental medicine to help eliminate excess fat. Zippy Salsa Shaker (page 199) blends daikon radishes with tomato, jalapeño, and other ingredients for great flavor. Also, dandelion leaves, juniper berries, alfalfa sprouts, and thyme have properties that aid in excretion of excess water as well as helping with detoxification, which is another weight-loss facilitator.

One last tip: Keep your colon healthy and functioning well. When waste sits in your colon for longer than normal (constipation), your body will absorb excess fat and toxins. This contributes to weight gain. Keep your elimination process regular with foods like prunes, still one of the best natural laxatives; see Colon Care, page 137. Also, you can add flaxseed or flaxseed oil to many of the smoothies and it won't affect the taste at all, but it will help your colon as well as your heart, skin, and hair. Be sure to get enough fiber, too, especially from whole grains; see the Meals-in-a-Glass section (pages 72–87). Also, fruits like apples contain soluble fibers such as pectin that are helpful for your colon. And don't forget to drink lots of water—at least eight glasses a day for a healthy colon and to facilitate weight loss.

Slim and Trim Shake

Total Weight:	24.0 oz.	Serving Size:	12.0 oz.

Serves 2

Basic Components

Calories	246.2
Calories from fat	128.4
Protein	2.3 g
Carbohydrates	34.1 g
Dietary fiber	2.4 g
Sugar—total	30.1 g
Fat—total	14.3 g
Saturated fat	2.3 g
Monounsaturated fat	1.7 g
Polyunsaturated fat	6.3 g

Vitamins

A—beta-carotene	2683.3 mcg
Vitamin B6	0.2 mg
Vitamin C	596.6 mg
Vitamin E	3.6 IU
Folate	42.7 mcg

Minerals

Calcium	29.7 mg
Iron	0.7 mg
Magnesium	29.7 mg
Potassium	443.4 mg
Selenium	0.7 mcg
Sodium	5.7 mg
Zinc	0.3 mg

Other Fats

Omega-3 fatty acids	0.8 g
Omega-6 fatty acids	5.5 g

Slim and Trim Shake

This is your grapefruit juice and breakfast—all in one glass! If you want this smoothie to be sweeter, cut off most of the white part of the grapefruit along with the skin, but be aware that you will also lose a lot of the nutrients.

Nutrisip: Grapefruit is low in calories and also helps lower cholesterol; it's high in vitamin C and flavonoids, especially the white part. Lecithin increases the solubility of cholesterol and aids in removal of cholesterol from tissue deposits.

Juice of 1 grapefruit, peeled before juicing if using a juice machine
Juice of 1 orange, peeled before juicing if using a juice machine
1 mango, peeled and cut into chunks from the pit
1 tablespoon soy lecithin granules
2 teaspoons bee pollen
1/2 teaspoon ascorbic acid (vitamin C powder)
6 ice cubes

Pour the juices into a blender and add the mango, lecithin, bee pollen, ascorbic acid, and ice. Blend on high speed until smooth and serve immediately.

Tomato Lemon Twist

Total Weight:	15.0 oz.	Serving Size:	7.5 oz.

Serves 2

Basic Components

Calories	40.0	Vitamin E	2.1 IU
Calories from fat	3.3	Folate	36.5 mcg
Protein	1.8 g	**Minerals**	
Carbohydrates	11.1 g	Calcium	34.2 mg
Dietary fiber	3.1 g	Iron	1.2 mg
Sugar—total	6.2 g	Magnesium	24.8 mg
Fat—total	0.4 g	Potassium	452.6 mg
Saturated fat	0.1 g	Selenium	0.9 mcg
Monounsaturated fat	0.1 g	Sodium	18.7 mg
Polyunsaturated fat	0.1 g	Zinc	0.3 mg
Vitamins		**Other Fats**	
A—beta-carotene	663.8 mcg	Omega-3 fatty acids	0.0 g
Vitamin B6	0.2 mg	Omega-6 fatty acids	0.1 g
Vitamin C	56.4 mg		

Tomato Lemon Twist

A terrific skinny sipper smoothie! Sip it for lunch for a very low cal meal.

Nutrisip: Tomatoes and lemon are rich in vitamin C and bioflavonoids, two nutrients that work together to support the immune system. Vitamin C levels in the body decrease with age, so the older we get, the more vitamin C–rich foods we should eat.

2 tomatoes, cut in chunks
1 cup tomato juice (2–3 medium tomatoes, juiced)
1/2 lemon, juiced, peeled if using a juice machine
1 teaspoon freshly grated lemon rind, preferably organic
6 fresh basil leaves, rinsed

Place the tomato chunks in a freezer bag and freeze them until solid. Pour the tomato juice into a blender and add the frozen tomato chunks, lemon juice, lemon peel, and basil. Blend on high speed until smooth and serve immediately.

Icy Spicy Tomato

Total Weight:	18.2 oz.	Serving Size:	9.1 oz.

Serves 2

Basic Components

Calories	57.6	Vitamin E	0.5 IU
Calories from fat	4.4	Folate	19.9 mcg
Protein	1.7 g	**Minerals**	
Carbohydrates	14.7 g	Calcium	44.6 mg
Dietary fiber	1.3 g	Iron	0.5 mg
Sugar—total	4.0 g	Magnesium	12.7 mg
Fat—total	0.5 g	Potassium	510.0 mg
Saturated fat	0.1 g	Selenium	0.4 mcg
Monounsaturated fat	0.0 g	Sodium	464.7 mg
Polyunsaturated fat	0.2 g	Zinc	0.1 mg
Vitamins		**Other Fats**	
A—beta-carotene	2088.8 mcg	Omega-3 fatty acids	0.0 g
Vitamin B6	0.1 mg	Omega-6 fatty acids	0.2 g
Vitamin C	52.2 mg		

Icy Spicy Tomato

A super calorie saver.

Nutrisip: Chili peppers actually induce the brain to secrete endorphins, those brain chemicals that are credited with the "runner's high." Endorphins block pain sensations and induce a kind of euphoria. When you're feeling great, you're less likely to go on a food binge and pack on the pounds. Also, radishes are known to stimulate the thyroid, and an efficient thyroid is a key to weight loss and maintenance.

2 tomatoes, cut in chunks
1 cup fresh carrot juice (about 5–7 carrots)
1/2 lemon, juiced, peeled if using a juice machine
2 tablespoons cilantro, rinsed and chopped
1/4 teaspoon sea salt
1/4 teaspoon ground cumin
1/4 small jalapeño, chopped, or to taste
3 radishes, washed and chopped

Place the tomato chunks in a freezer bag and freeze them until solid. Pour the carrot and lemon juices into a blender and add the frozen tomato chunks, cilantro, salt, cumin, jalapeño, and radishes. Blend on high speed until smooth and serve immediately.

Island Breeze

Total Weight:	17.2 oz.	Serving Size:	8.6 oz.

Serves 2

BASIC COMPONENTS			
Calories	119.6	Vitamin E	2.4 IU
Calories from fat	4.6	Folate	19.1 mcg
Protein	1.3 g	MINERALS	
Carbohydrates	30.8 g	Calcium	13.9 mg
Dietary fiber	2.3 g	Iron	0.4 mg
Sugar—total	25.9 g	Magnesium	12.3 mg
Fat—total	0.5 g	Potassium	360.9 mg
Saturated fat	0.1 g	Selenium	1.1 mcg
Monounsaturated fat	0.1 g	Sodium	6.3 mg
Polyunsaturated fat	0.1 g	Zinc	0.2 mg
VITAMINS		OTHER FATS	
A—beta-carotene	2415.7 mcg	Omega-3 fatty acids	0.0 g
Vitamin B6	0.2 mg	Omega-6 fatty acids	0.1 g
Vitamin C	33.4 mg		

Island Breeze

Through the years I've often been asked if one can juice a pomegranate. You can juice or blend the seeds, but the white membrane has a very bitter taste and should be removed. Pomegranate blends an interesting flavor with the sweet mango.

Nutrisip: Mango is a good source of beta-carotene, or provitamin A, a precursor from which your body can make vitamin A. Beta-carotene is very susceptible to oxidation (a result of exposure to light and air), so drink your carotene-rich smoothie right after you make it.

1 ripe mango, peeled and cut in chunks from the pit
*3/4 cup pomegranate seeds (remove all membranes)**
6 ice cubes

Place the mango, pomegranate seeds, and ice in a blender and process on high speed until smooth. Serve immediately.

**If you don't have a pomegranate for this recipe, blend in the same amount of diced pineapple or orange.*

Madame Butterfly

Total Weight:	17.6 oz.	Serving Size:	8.8 oz.

Serves 2

BASIC COMPONENTS

Calories	73.8
Calories from fat	2.4
Protein	0.9 g
Carbohydrates	17.9 g
Dietary fiber	2.3 g
Sugar—total	15.5 g
Fat—total	0.3 g
Saturated fat	0.0 g
Monounsaturated fat	0.1 g
Polyunsaturated fat	0.1 g
VITAMINS	
A—beta-carotene	7.2 mcg
Vitamin B6	0.1 mg
Vitamin C	49.3 mg
Vitamin E	0.6 IU
Folate	17.5 mcg
MINERALS	
Calcium	13.6 mg
Iron	0.3 mg
Magnesium	19.7 mg
Potassium	273.9 mg
Selenium	0.5 mcg
Sodium	1.2 mg
Zinc	0.1 mg
OTHER FATS	
Omega-3 fatty acids	0.0 g
Omega-6 fatty acids	0.1 g

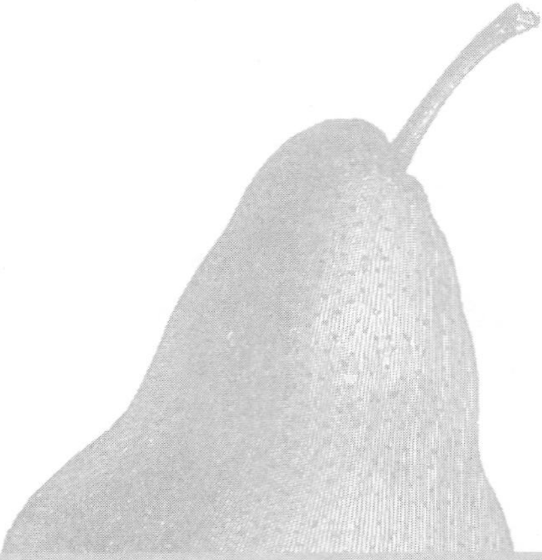

Madame Butterfly

This is a very light, refreshing smoothie. It also makes a delicious sorbet; see Green Tea Pear Sorbet (page 307).

Nutrisip: Green tea has been shown in studies to have cancer-preventative properties. In Japan there is strong supporting evidence that regular green-tea drinkers have dramatically lower rates of stomach cancer.

6 green tea ice cubes
1 cup white grape juice (2 cups green grapes, juiced)
1 medium pear, washed, stem removed, and cut into chunks

Steep one bag of green tea in a cup of hot water for about 20 minutes, or until the tea is strong and flavorful. Pour it into six ice cube tray squares and freeze. Pour the grape juice into a blender and add the pear and green tea ice cubes. Blend on high speed until smooth and serve immediately.

Just Peachy and Spice

Total Weight:	20.2 oz.	Serving Size:	10.1 oz.

Serves 2

Basic Components

Calories	94.3	Vitamin E	0.1 IU
Calories from fat	7.2	Folate	28.9 mcg
Protein	2.5 g	**Minerals**	
Carbohydrates	20.9 g	Calcium	19.9 mg
Dietary fiber	2.9 g	Iron	0.6 mg
Sugar—total	18.6 g	Magnesium	17.5 mg
Fat—total	0.8 g	Potassium	427.2 mg
Saturated fat	0.1 g	Selenium	0.5 mcg
Monounsaturated fat	0.1 g	Sodium	6.8 mg
Polyunsaturated fat	0.3 g	Zinc	0.2 mg
Vitamins		**Other Fats**	
A—beta-carotene	84.7 mcg	Omega-3 fatty acids	0.0 g
Vitamin B6	0.1 mg	Omega-6 fatty acids	0.3 g
Vitamin C	52.7 mg		

Just Peachy and Spice

A fabulous midday pick-me-up.

Nutrisip: Since ancient times, cinnamon has been used as a medicine to treat colds, warm digestion, and ease flatulence.

3/4 cup orange juice (3 oranges, peeled and juiced)
1-inch chunk gingerroot, juiced or grated
1/4 cup plain soy milk or milk of choice
2 ripe peaches, rinsed, skin and pit removed, and cut into chunks
1/2 teaspoon ground cinnamon
6 ice cubes

Pour the orange juice and ginger juice or grated ginger and milk into a blender and add the peaches, cinnamon, and ice. Blend on high speed until smooth and serve immediately.

All That Razz

Total Weight: 13.6 oz. Serving Size: 6.8 oz.

Serves 2

BASIC COMPONENTS

Calories	64.2
Calories from fat	4.3
Protein	1.1 g
Carbohydrates	15.2 g
Dietary fiber	3.2 g
Sugar—total	11.1 g
Fat—total	0.5 g
Saturated fat	0.0 g
Monounsaturated fat	0.0 g
Polyunsaturated fat	0.1 g
VITAMINS	
A—beta-carotene	30.6 mcg
Vitamin B6	0.0 mg
Vitamin C	67.2 mg
Vitamin E	0.3 IU
Folate	14.3 mcg
MINERALS	
Calcium	28.6 mg
Iron	0.5 mg
Magnesium	13.6 mg
Potassium	266.8 mg
Selenium	0.3 mcg
Sodium	2.5 mg
Zinc	0.2 mg
OTHER FATS	
Omega-3 fatty acids	0.0 g
Omega-6 fatty acids	0.1 g

All That Razz

Fruit and ice—there's virtually no fat, just great flavor.

Nutrisip: This smoothie is loaded with vitamin C and bioflavonoids—two nutrients that strengthen blood vessel walls and help prevent easy bruising.

1/2 cup white grape juice (1 cup green grapes, juiced)
1/2 cup fresh or frozen raspberries, rinsed if fresh
1 kiwifruit, peeled and chopped into chunks
6 ice cubes

Pour the grape juice into a blender and add the berries, kiwi, and ice. Blend on high speed until smooth and serve immediately.

Zippy Salsa Shaker

Total Weight:	49.2 oz.	Serving Size:	24.6 oz.

Serves 2

BASIC COMPONENTS

Calories	121.4	Vitamin E	1.1 IU
Calories from fat	8.6	Folate	130.4 mcg
Protein	5.5 g	MINERALS	
Carbohydrates	28.2 g	Calcium	106.5 mg
Dietary fiber	7.7 g	Iron	2.2 mg
Sugar—total	15.6 g	Magnesium	77.8 mg
Fat—total	1.0 g	Potassium	1731.7 mg
Saturated fat	0.2 g	Selenium	3.2 mcg
Monounsaturated fat	0.2 g	Sodium	174.0 mg
Polyunsaturated fat	0.4 g	Zinc	0.7 mg
VITAMINS		OTHER FATS	
A—beta-carotene	688.4 mcg	Omega-3 fatty acids	0.1 g
Vitamin B6	0.3 mg	Omega-6 fatty acids	0.3 g
Vitamin C	171.8 mg		

Zippy Salsa Shaker

If you like salsa, try this shake.

Nutrisip: Lycopene is an antioxidant that gives the tomato its bright red color. It has been noted to be twice as powerful an antioxidant as beta-carotene. Daikon radish has been used in traditional Oriental medicine to help eliminate excess fats.

2 cups tomato, cut in chunks
1 cup fresh cucumber juice (1/2 cucumber, peeled if not organic, and juiced, or peeled, cut in chunks, and frozen)
1 lemon, juiced, peeled if using a juice machine
1/2 teaspoon freshly grated lemon peel, preferably organic
2 daikon radishes, washed
Dash cayenne pepper

Place tomato chunks (and cucumber if freezing) in a freezer bag and freeze them until solid. Pour the cucumber juice or chunks and the lemon juice into a blender and add the frozen tomato chunks, lemon peel, daikon radishes, and cayenne. Blend on high speed until smooth and serve immediately.

Spicy Tropical Squeeze

Total Weight:	18.2 oz.	Serving Size:	9.1 oz.

Serves 2

Basic Components

Calories	92.6
Calories from fat	2.0
Protein	1.0 g
Carbohydrates	22.6 g
Dietary fiber	2.8 g
Sugar—total	15.0 g
Fat—total	0.2 g
Saturated fat	0.1 g
Monounsaturated fat	0.1 g
Polyunsaturated fat	0.1 g

Vitamins

A—beta-carotene	98.8 mcg
Vitamin B6	0.0 mg
Vitamin C	109.0 mg
Vitamin E	2.5 IU
Folate	57.9 mcg

Minerals

Calcium	37.6 mg
Iron	0.2 mg
Magnesium	16.2 mg
Potassium	473.3 mg
Selenium	0.9 mcg
Sodium	8.5 mg
Zinc	0.1 mg

Other Fats

Omega-3 fatty acids	0.0 g
Omega-6 fatty acids	0.0 g

Spicy Tropical Squeeze

Ginger for zest, papaya for richness, and pineapple for sweetness—superdelicious!

Nutrisip: Ginger is a spice that has been shown to lower cholesterol. It also has thermogenic properties, meaning it facilitates energy production, which can promote weight loss.

1/2 cup pineapple juice (juice about 1/4 pineapple and its core; or cut in chunks)
1-inch chunk gingerroot, juiced or grated
1 cup papaya, peeled, seeded, and cut into chunks
4 ice cubes

Pour the pineapple juice and ginger juice (or grated ginger) into a blender and add the papaya and ice cubes. Blend on high speed until smooth and serve immediately.

Healthful Smoothies, Shakes, and Popsicles Kids Love

Smoothies are far superior to soda pop or sugary powdered drinks, especially for children. Soda pop contains phosphates, which bind calcium—a mineral that is greatly needed by your child for good teeth and bone formation. Soda pop and powdered drink mixes are laden with sugars (either refined or artificial) and chemicals, neither of which is healthful. Diet sodas are even worse because they are usually sweetened with aspartame (popularly known as NutraSweet), which contains phenylalanine and aspartic acid. Critics of this artificial sweetener say that high concentrations of phenylalanine can cause mental retardation in some children, and aspartic acid in high doses can act as a neurotoxin, promoting hormonal disorders (*Nutrition Week,* 1995).*

A two-year study by the U.S. Department of Agriculture in 1989 showed that nearly one-quarter of all vegetables consumed by children and adolescents

*To get a copy of the four-page FDA report "Summary of Adverse Reactions Attributable to Aspartame," send a stamped, self-addressed envelope to Centers for Nutrition Information, 910 17th Street NW, Suite 413, Washington, D.C. 20006.

were French fries. Only one in five children ate five or more servings of fruits and vegetables per day. An "Eat-Your-Vegetables" Smoothie (page 215) is one way to get more vegetables into your child's diet; most children like smoothies, and the delicious fruit smoothies will help them down their fruit servings easily. Best of all for you, they only take minutes to make.

Between 1989 and 1991 it was found that only 45 percent of the four- to six-year-olds studied and 32 percent of the seven- to ten-year-olds consumed adequate amounts of fiber, which put them at risk for future chronic diseases (*Journal of the American Dietetic Association,* 1998). High-fiber foods include fruits, vegetables, seeds, nuts, legumes, and whole grains. Fresh fruit, seeds, or nuts can increase the fiber in your child's diet as you blend up these ingredients in yummy drinks.

Fresh-fruit smoothies like Off-to-School Brain Power (page 205) make an ideal breakfast-in-a-glass on busy days. Also, see the section Meals-in-a-Glass (page 72) for more breakfast ideas. After-School Pick-Me-Up (page 209) offers a healthy midday snack, and Terrific Homework Helper (page 217) provides electrolytes that energize the body and choline to improve brain functions.

Don't forget that desserts and treats should also be as healthful as possible. You can make delicious homemade popsicles with blended fruit without any extra sugar or artificial ingredients. Also, try some of the natural desserts in Just Desserts (page 304) for a yummy alternative to ice cream.

Off-to-School Brain Power

Total Weight:	20.0 oz.	Serving Size:	10.0 oz.

Serves 2

Basic Components

Calories	192.8	Vitamin E	0.9 IU
Calories from fat	83.0	Folate	45.8 mcg
Protein	5.8 g	**Minerals**	
Carbohydrates	24.9 g	Calcium	132.1 mg
Dietary fiber	3.2 g	Iron	2.5 mg
Sugar—total	20.2 g	Magnesium	22.2 mg
Fat—total	9.2 g	Potassium	332.1 mg
Saturated fat	2.4 g	Selenium	2.4 mcg
Monounsaturated fat	1.4 g	Sodium	62.8 mg
Polyunsaturated fat	3.3 g	Zinc	0.7 mg
Vitamins		**Other Fats**	
A—beta-carotene	32.2 mcg	Omega-3 fatty acids	0.4 g
Vitamin B6	0.2 mg	Omega-6 fatty acids	2.8 g
Vitamin C	71.1 mg		

Off-to-School Brain Power

A fast, delicious smoothie to start your child's day right! The strawberry-orange flavor makes it appealing. Lecithin actually doesn't have any flavor; it picks up the flavor of the fruit, but check out what it does for the brain.

Nutrisip: Acetylcholine is the most important neurotransmitter for memory and intelligence, and the body makes it from choline, a B-complex vitamin. Some studies show that choline has improved memory dramatically in healthy young adults. There is some evidence that choline can improve mental functioning and thought transmission by strengthening neurons in the brain's memory centers. Lecithin is one of the best sources of choline; oranges are also a fairly good source.

1/2 cup plain nonfat yogurt
1 orange, peeled, cut into chunks
1 cup fresh or frozen strawberries, caps removed and rinsed, if fresh (8–10 strawberries)
1 tablespoon lecithin granules
1 tablespoon protein powder
1 tablespoon honey, optional
1 teaspoon pure vanilla extract
6–8 ice cubes

Combine the yogurt in a blender with the orange, strawberries, lecithin, protein powder, honey as desired, vanilla, and ice. Blend on high speed until smooth. Serve immediately.

Orange Coconut Creamsicle-in-a-Glass

Total Weight:	21.6 oz.	Serving Size:	10.8 oz.

Serves 2

BASIC COMPONENTS

Calories	250.6
Calories from fat	120.2
Protein	5.9 g
Carbohydrates	29.4 g
Dietary fiber	7.9 g
Sugar—total	20.8 g
Fat—total	13.4 g
Saturated fat	9.9 g
Monounsaturated fat	0.9 g
Polyunsaturated fat	1.2 g

VITAMINS

A—beta-carotene	46.9 mcg
Vitamin B6	0.2 mg
Vitamin C	81.3 mg
Vitamin E	0.6 IU
Folate	57.7 mcg

MINERALS

Calcium	65.9 mg
Iron	1.7 mg
Magnesium	47.8 mg
Potassium	541.3 mg
Selenium	6.2 mcg
Sodium	23.0 mg
Zinc	0.7 mg

OTHER FATS

Omega-3 fatty acids	0.1 g
Omega-6 fatty acids	1.0 g

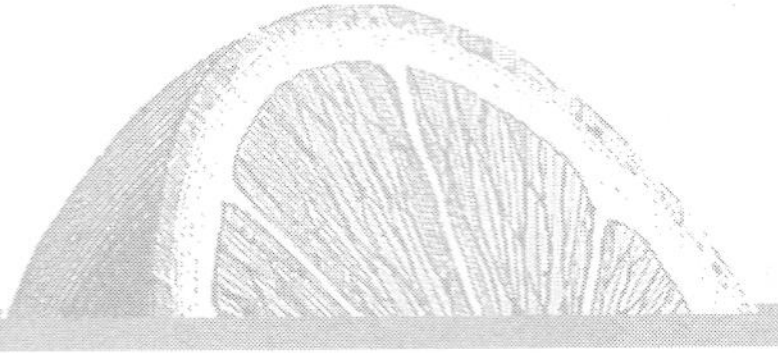

Orange Coconut Creamsicle-in-a-Glass

Really delicious!

Nutrisip: Soy and oranges are good sources of calcium, which is necessary for healthy bone and tooth formation. Now you can tell your kids that drinking their calcium is fun.

1 cup plain soy milk or milk of choice
2 oranges, peeled, cut into chunks, and juiced or added directly to the blender
1/2 cup grated coconut, lightly packed
2 teaspoons pure vanilla extract
2 teaspoons honey
6 ice cubes

Pour the milk and orange juice (or orange chunks) into a blender and add the coconut, vanilla, honey, and ice. Blend on high speed until smooth. Serve immediately.

After-School Pick-Me-Up

Total Weight:	22.6 oz.	Serving Size:	11.3 oz.

Serves 2

BASIC COMPONENTS

Calories	188.3
Calories from fat	11.0
Protein	2.6 g
Carbohydrates	45.9 g
Dietary fiber	3.5 g
Sugar—total	40.9 g
Fat—total	1.2 g
Saturated fat	0.3 g
Monounsaturated fat	0.2 g
Polyunsaturated fat	0.3 g
VITAMINS	
A—beta-carotene	471.3 mcg
Vitamin B6	0.5 mg
Vitamin C	75.2 mg
Vitamin E	1.2 IU
Folate	54.7 mcg
MINERALS	
Calcium	33.9 mg
Iron	1.0 mg
Magnesium	41.3 mg
Potassium	688.7 mg
Selenium	1.2 mcg
Sodium	3.8 mg
Zinc	0.3 mg
OTHER FATS	
Omega-3 fatty acids	0.1 g
Omega-6 fatty acids	0.2 g

After-School Pick-Me-Up

This energy enhancer beats soda pop in flavor, and it's so much better for growing bodies!

Nutrisip: Grapes and oranges are good sources of selenium, a mineral that can help relieve fatigue and energize the body after a hard day of study and schoolwork.

1 cup orange juice (2 oranges, juiced, peeled if using a juice machine)
3/4 cup red grapes, juiced, or 1/4 cup red grape juice
1 cup frozen unsweetened cherries
1 frozen banana, cut in chunks

Pour the orange juice and grape juice into a blender and add the cherries and banana. Blend on high speed until smooth. Serve immediately.

Peanut Butter Banana Flip

Total Weight:	18.6 oz.	Serving Size:	9.3 oz.

Serves 2

Basic Components

Calories	194.2	Vitamin E	2.6 IU
Calories from fat	97.1	Folate	25.0 mcg
Protein	8.0 g	**Minerals**	
Carbohydrates	19.2 g	Calcium	15.8 mg
Dietary fiber	4.0 g	Iron	1.2 mg
Sugar—total	12.5 g	Magnesium	66.5 mg
Fat—total	10.8 g	Potassium	513.4 mg
Saturated fat	2.0 g	Selenium	3.4 mcg
Monounsaturated fat	4.3 g	Sodium	92.0 mg
Polyunsaturated fat	3.3 g	Zinc	0.9 mg
Vitamins		**Other Fats**	
A—beta-carotene	28.3 mcg	Omega-3 fatty acids	0.2 g
Vitamin B6	0.5 mg	Omega-6 fatty acids	3.1 g
Vitamin C	5.4 mg		

Peanut Butter Banana Flip

Now tell me, what kid doesn't like peanut butter and banana together!

Nutrisip: This smoothie is packed with potassium (bananas, soy, and peanut butter). Potassium is called an electrolyte because it carries a small positive electrical charge and plays a key role in energy metabolism in the body. Fatigue and exhaustion are associated with low potassium levels. The next time your child is too tired to do homework, energize him or her with this smoothie.

1 cup soy milk or milk of choice
2 tablespoons natural peanut butter, creamy or crunchy
1 teaspoon pure vanilla extract
1 frozen banana, cut into chunks
6 ice cubes

Pour the milk into a blender and add the peanut butter, vanilla, banana, and ice. Blend on high speed until smooth and serve immediately.

Choose natural peanut butter that contains only peanuts and salt. Avoid peanut butter that has hydrogenated oils, sugar or other sweeteners, or any other fillers. Natural peanut butter is the healthiest choice, and it tastes just as good, if not better, than the other varieties.

Shake-Me-Up Melon

Total Weight: 13.2 oz. Serving Size: 6.6 oz.

Serves 2

BASIC COMPONENTS

Calories	81.1
Calories from fat	4.2
Protein	1.5 g
Carbohydrates	19.5 g
Dietary fiber	1.1 g
Sugar—total	18.2 g
Fat—total	0.5 g
Saturated fat	0.1 g
Monounsaturated fat	0.0 g
Polyunsaturated fat	0.2 g

VITAMINS

A—beta-carotene	2328.3 mcg
Vitamin B6	0.2 mg
Vitamin C	82.3 mg
Vitamin E	0.4 IU
Folate	39.4 mcg

MINERALS

Calcium	21.0 mg
Iron	0.4 mg
Magnesium	20.2 mg
Potassium	497.7 mg
Selenium	0.6 mcg
Sodium	11.6 mg
Zinc	0.2 mg

OTHER FATS

Omega-3 fatty acids	0.1 g
Omega-6 fatty acids	0.1 g

Shake-Me-Up Melon

A refreshing shake any time of day.

Nutrisip: Cantaloupe is rich in beta-carotene, an antioxidant that strengthens the immune system, improving a child's resistance to infections, especially those in the respiratory system.

1/2 cup orange juice (about 1 orange, juiced, peeled if using a juice machine)
1 1/2 cups frozen cantaloupe chunks
1/2 teaspoon grated orange peel, preferably organic
1 teaspoon honey

Pour the orange juice into a blender and add the frozen cantaloupe, orange peel, and honey. Blend on high speed until smooth and serve immediately.

Honey should not be fed to children under the age of two—even pasteurized honey. It can transmit heat-resistant bacteria spores that can cause botulism. The mature intestines of older children and adults can handle these spores, but the intestines of a small child cannot. Omit honey from any recipes in this book when serving a child under two years old. Actually, little children don't need extra sweeteners; their taste buds are immature. Fruit has enough natural sweetness. And if you start them out without a lot of sweets, they may not want a lot of them when they're older.

"Eat-Your-Vegetables" Smoothie

Total Weight: 22.6 oz. Serving Size: 11.3 oz.

Serves 2

BASIC COMPONENTS

Calories	265.7
Calories from fat	146.4
Protein	6.5 g
Carbohydrates	28.7 g
Dietary fiber	2.2 g
Sugar—total	13.9 g
Fat—total	16.3 g
Saturated fat	3.2 g
Monounsaturated fat	9.4 g
Polyunsaturated fat	2.8 g
VITAMINS	
A—beta-carotene	841.9 mcg
Vitamin B6	0.2 mg
Vitamin C	28.5 mg
Vitamin E	0.4 IU
Folate	28.8 mcg
MINERALS	
Calcium	53.5 mg
Iron	2.5 mg
Magnesium	98.6 mg
Potassium	624.5 mg
Selenium	4.3 mcg
Sodium	72.5 mg
Zinc	2.0 mg
OTHER FATS	
Omega-3 fatty acids	0.1 g
Omega-6 fatty acids	2.7 g

"Eat-Your-Vegetables" Smoothie

I did a version of this smoothie—Popeye's Power Drink—for my Juice Lady Infomercial and forty six- to ten-year-olds tasted it. They loved it! So will your child.

Nutrisip: Children should eat five to nine servings of fruits and vegetables each day, and the vegetables (three to five servings) can be quite a challenge to sell your child. But kids love juice and smoothies, so why not turn some of those vegetable servings into a delicious smoothie?

2/3 cup fresh carrot juice (3–5 medium carrots, juiced)
1/2 cup fresh apple juice (about 1 1/2 apples, juiced)
1/4 lemon, juiced, peeled if using a juice machine
1/4 cup spinach, washed well, juiced
1/2 cup pineapple chunks
1/2 cup raw cashews
6 ice cubes

Pour the carrot, apple, lemon, and spinach juices into a blender and add the pineapple chunks, cashews, and ice. Blend on high speed until smooth. Serve immediately.

Terrific Homework Helper

Total Weight:	19.2 oz.	Serving Size:	9.6 oz.

Serves 2

Basic Components

Calories	146.4	Vitamin E	0.9 IU
Calories from fat	69.3	Folate	17.3 mcg
Protein	3.3 g	**Minerals**	
Carbohydrates	21.2 g	Calcium	14.0 mg
Dietary fiber	3.4 g	Iron	0.5 mg
Sugar—total	15.2 g	Magnesium	25.1 mg
Fat—total	7.7 g	Potassium	862.9 mg
Saturated fat	1.2 g	Selenium	1.2 mcg
Monounsaturated fat	0.9 g	Sodium	107.8 mg
Polyunsaturated fat	3.4 g	Zinc	0.2 mg
Vitamins		**Other Fats**	
A—beta-carotene	54.1 mcg	Omega-3 fatty acids	0.4 g
Vitamin B6	0.4 mg	Omega-6 fatty acids	3.0 g
Vitamin C	292.2 mg		

Terrific Homework Helper

This smoothie has a pretty mint-green color, but the best part is that it tastes terrific!

Nutrisip: Loaded with potassium, calcium, and phosphorus, this smoothie offers important electrolytes that contribute to energy and endurance. It also supplies a wallop of choline, the amazing brain energizer and memory enhancer. The body normally produces enough choline for neurotransmitter production, but when nerve cells are stressed, as can happen with school tests, activities, and homework, the need for acetylcholine can outpace choline production. Lecithin is the best source of choline, but it's also found in soy, peanut butter, and spinach.

1 cup spinach, washed, juiced
1/2 medium or 1 small apple, washed, juiced
1 celery stalk, washed, juiced
1/4 cup plain soy milk
1 tablespoon peanut butter, creamy or crunchy
1 tablespoon lecithin granules
1/4 teaspoon ascorbic acid (vitamin C powder)
1 frozen banana, cut into chunks

Pour the spinach, apple, and celery juices into a blender and add the soy milk, peanut butter, lecithin, ascorbic acid, and banana. Blend on high speed until smooth and serve immediately.

Go Bananas!

To freeze a banana, always peel first. If you freeze a banana with the skin on, it will be quite a chore to get the peel off once it's frozen. Wrap the peeled banana in plastic wrap or place in a baggy and store in the freezer until ready to use. Bananas can be stored in the freezer several weeks.

Tummy Ache Reliever

Total Weight:	12.1 oz.	Serving Size:	12.1 oz.

Serves 1

Basic Components

Calories	132.1
Calories from fat	33.6
Protein	6.0 g
Carbohydrates	19.1 g
Dietary fiber	5.4 g
Sugar—total	9.5 g
Fat—total	3.7 g
Saturated fat	0.5 g
Monounsaturated fat	0.7 g
Polyunsaturated fat	1.6 g

Vitamins

A—beta-carotene	83.1 mcg
Vitamin B6	0.1 mg
Vitamin C	98.0 mg
Vitamin E	2.6 IU
Folate	61.4 mcg

Minerals

Calcium	48.7 mg
Iron	1.2 mg
Magnesium	50.8 mg
Potassium	656.1 mg
Selenium	3.3 mcg
Sodium	26.8 mg
Zinc	0.5 mg

Other Fats

Omega-3 fatty acids	0.2 g
Omega-6 fatty acids	1.4 g

Tummy Ache Reliever

Tastes like a Dreamsicle; comforts like a teddy bear!

Nutrisip: Papaya contains the enzyme papain, which is a protein-digesting enzyme that relieves gas and bloating.

*3/4 cup plain soy milk or milk of choice **
1 small papaya, peeled, seeded, cut into chunks, and frozen (about 1 1/2 cups)
1 1/2 teaspoons freshly grated orange peel, preferably organic
1 teaspoon pure vanilla extract

Pour the milk into a blender and add the papaya, orange peel, and vanilla. Blend on high speed until smooth and serve immediately.

**Omit dairy milk if stomach pain occurs often; your child could be allergic to this food. See below.*

Be aware that allergies to milk, wheat, eggs, or other allergens can cause intestinal discomfort such as stomach pain, nausea, bloating, gas, belching, and bad breath. If your child continually complains of stomach aches or has any of these other symptoms, he or she may be experiencing an allergic reaction to dairy milk or other commonly eaten foods. Try soy milk instead of dairy milk, and alternative grains, to wheat. Also, look for a doctor who can test for food allergies.

Hawaiian Sunrise Popsicles

Total Weight: 17.4 oz. Serving Size: 2.9 oz.

Makes 6

BASIC COMPONENTS

Calories	70.9
Calories from fat	24.1
Protein	0.6 g
Carbohydrates	12.6 g
Dietary fiber	1.3 g
Sugar—total	11.1 g
Fat—total	2.7 g
Saturated fat	2.2 g
Monounsaturated fat	0.1 g
Polyunsaturated fat	0.1 g

VITAMINS

A—beta-carotene	13.7 mcg
Vitamin B6	0.1 mg
Vitamin C	18.6 mg
Vitamin E	0.2 IU
Folate	13.7 mcg

MINERALS

Calcium	7.1 mg
Iron	0.4 mg
Magnesium	11.9 mg
Potassium	127.3 mg
Selenium	1.1 mcg
Sodium	2.3 mg
Zinc	0.1 mg

OTHER FATS

Omega-3 fatty acids	0.0 g
Omega-6 fatty acids	0.1 g

Hawaiian Sunrise Popsicles

A delicious tropical treat!

Nutrisip: Coconut contains manganese, a mineral that contributes to healthy skin, hair, and nails—so important for growing bodies.

1/2 cup orange juice (1 orange, juiced, peeled if using a juice machine)
2 cups fresh pineapple, cubed
1/3 cup grated coconut, lightly packed
1 tablespoon honey

Pour the orange juice into a blender and add the pineapple, coconut, and honey. Blend on high speed until smooth, pour into six 3-ounce popsicle molds, and freeze.

When using popsicle molds for the first time, wash them with hot soapy water and rinse. Pour clear water into the molds and let it stand overnight to release any solvents in the plastic that remain from the manufacturing process. In the morning, pour out the water and rinse the molds well.

Purple Power Pops

Total Weight:	16.8 oz.	Serving Size:	2.8 oz.

Makes 6

Basic Components

Calories	47.6	Vitamin E	0.9 IU
Calories from fat	2.6	Folate	4.3 mcg
Protein	0.5 g	**Minerals**	
Carbohydrates	12.1 g	Calcium	7.2 mg
Dietary fiber	1.6 g	Iron	0.2 mg
Sugar—total	10.4 g	Magnesium	4.0 mg
Fat—total	0.3 g	Potassium	101.6 mg
Saturated fat	0.1 g	Selenium	0.4 mcg
Monounsaturated fat	0.0 g	Sodium	3.5 mg
Polyunsaturated fat	0.1 g	Zinc	0.1 mg
Vitamins		**Other Fats**	
A—beta-carotene	47.1 mcg	Omega-3 fatty acids	0.0 g
Vitamin B6	0.1 mg	Omega-6 fatty acids	0.1 g
Vitamin C	7.5 mg		

Purple Power Pops

If your kids like grape juice, they'll love this popsicle.

Nutrisip: Grapes are rich in bioflavonoids, and strawberries are an excellent source of vitamin C. These two nutrients work together to build resistance to infections. Sugar weakens the immune system, but these nutrients strengthen it. The more you choose natural treats over sugar-sweetened snacks and desserts, the more your children should be able to resist colds, flu, and other illnesses.

2 cups red grapes, rinsed and picked from the stems

1 cup strawberries, rinsed, caps removed

Pour the grapes and strawberries into a blender and process on high speed until smooth. Pour the mixture into six 3-ounce popsicle molds and freeze.

Strawberry Creamsicles

Total Weight:	14.4 oz.	Serving Size:	2.4 oz.

Makes 6

BASIC COMPONENTS

Calories	28.3
Calories from fat	6.4
Protein	1.1 g
Carbohydrates	4.9 g
Dietary fiber	1.2 g
Sugar—total	3.6 g
Fat—total	0.7 g
Saturated fat	0.1 g
Monounsaturated fat	0.1 g
Polyunsaturated fat	0.3 g

VITAMINS

A—beta-carotene	5.6 mcg
Vitamin B6	0.0 mg
Vitamin C	19.5 mg
Vitamin E	0.1 IU
Folate	6.6 mcg

MINERALS

Calcium	6.2 mg
Iron	0.3 mg
Magnesium	9.3 mg
Potassium	101.4 mg
Selenium	0.7 mcg
Sodium	4.1 mg
Zinc	0.1 mg

OTHER FATS

Omega-3 fatty acids	0.1 g
Omega-6 fatty acids	0.3 g

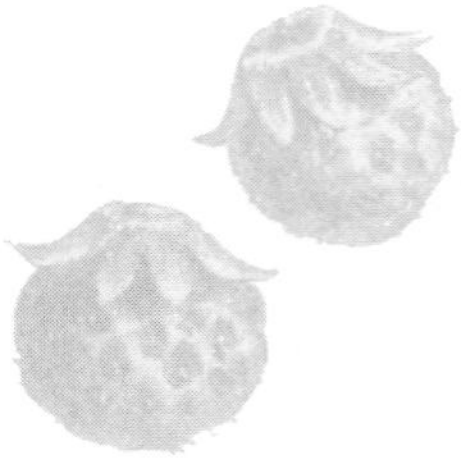

Strawberry Creamsicles

Pretty and pink.

Nutrisip: Strawberries are a good source of ellagic acid, a plant compound linked with anti-cancer properties. In one study, strawberries topped the list of eight foods most linked to the lowest cancer rates.

3/4 cup soy milk or milk of choice
1 cup strawberries, rinsed, caps removed
2 teaspoons honey
1/2 teaspoon pure vanilla extract
4–5 medium strawberries, rinsed, caps removed, and chopped

Pour the milk into a blender and add the whole strawberries, honey, and vanilla. Blend on high speed until smooth. Stir in the chopped strawberries. Pour the mixture into six 3-ounce popsicle molds and freeze.

Super Orange Champs

Total Weight: 15.2 oz. Serving Size: 1.9 oz.

Makes 6–8

BASIC COMPONENTS

Calories	50.5
Calories from fat	16.1
Protein	0.4 g
Carbohydrates	9.4 g
Dietary fiber	0.3 g
Sugar—total	8.9 g
Fat—total	1.8 g
Saturated fat	0.3 g
Monounsaturated fat	0.2 g
Polyunsaturated fat	0.8 g
VITAMINS	
A—beta-carotene	17.9 mcg
Vitamin B6	0.0 mg
Vitamin C	23.9 mg
Vitamin E	0.2 IU
Folate	14.4 mcg
MINERALS	
Calcium	8.1 mg
Iron	0.1 mg
Magnesium	5.2 mg
Potassium	95.3 mg
Selenium	0.1 mcg
Sodium	0.6 mg
Zinc	0.0 mg
OTHER FATS	
Omega-3 fatty acids	0.1 g
Omega-6 fatty acids	0.7 g

Super Orange Champs

Before children learn to appreciate flossing, this tasty treat can help between trips to the dentist.

Nutrisip: For healthy gums and good dental checkups, add more vitamin C– and bioflavonoid-rich foods like oranges to your child's diet.

1 1/4 cups orange juice (about 3 oranges, juiced, peeled if using a juice machine)
2 tablespoons honey
1 tablespoon lecithin granules
1/2 teaspoon freshly grated orange peel, preferably organic
1/2 orange, peeled and chopped into small pieces

Pour the orange juice into a blender and add the honey, lecithin, and orange peel. Blend on high speed until smooth. Stir in the orange pieces. Pour into six to eight 3-ounce popsicle molds and freeze.

Grape Juice Slide

Total Weight:	20.0 oz.	Serving Size:	2.5 oz.

Makes 8

BASIC COMPONENTS

Calories	34.5	Vitamin E	0.5 IU
Calories from fat	2.8	Folate	5.0 mcg
Protein	0.4 g	MINERALS	
Carbohydrates	8.5 g	Calcium	7.4 mg
Dietary fiber	0.9 g	Iron	0.2 mg
Sugar—total	7.6 g	Magnesium	4.5 mg
Fat—total	0.3 g	Potassium	107.6 mg
Saturated fat	0.1 g	Selenium	0.3 mcg
Monounsaturated fat	0.0 g	Sodium	1.3 mg
Polyunsaturated fat	0.1 g	Zinc	0.1 mg
VITAMINS		OTHER FATS	
A—beta-carotene	19.7 mcg	Omega-3 fatty acids	0.0 g
Vitamin B6	0.1 mg	Omega-6 fatty acids	0.1 g
Vitamin C	15.2 mg		

Grape Juice Slide

A pretty purple popsicle that's jump-up-and-down delicious.

Nutrisip: If your child has a sensitivity to bright lights, as I did when I was a child, add more blueberries to his or her diet. Post–World War II studies proved that bilberry (similar to blueberry) extracts improve nighttime vision and lead to quicker adjustment to darkness.

*2 cups purple grapes, rinsed and juiced (remove all large stems; small stems can be juiced)**

2 cups frozen or fresh blueberries, rinsed if fresh

Pour the grape juice into a blender and add the blueberries. Blend on high speed until smooth. Pour the mixture into eight 3-ounce popsicle molds and freeze.

**If you don't have a juice machine, pick all the grapes from their stems and blend.*

Jump-Up-and-Down Fudgsicles

Total Weight: 13.8 oz. Serving Size: 2.3 oz.

Makes 6

Basic Components

Calories	48.0
Calories from fat	7.9
Protein	1.4 g
Carbohydrates	9.1 g
Dietary fiber	1.3 g
Sugar—total	3.8 g
Fat—total	0.9 g
Saturated fat	0.1 g
Monounsaturated fat	0.1 g
Polyunsaturated fat	0.4 g
Vitamins	
A—beta-carotene	9.4 mcg
Vitamin B6	0.1 mg
Vitamin C	1.8 mg
Vitamin E	0.1 IU
Folate	4.4 mcg
Minerals	
Calcium	4.1 mg
Iron	0.5 mg
Magnesium	13.7 mg
Potassium	139.6 mg
Selenium	0.8 mcg
Sodium	9.2 mg
Zinc	0.1 mg
Other Fats	
Omega-3 fatty acids	0.1 g
Omega-6 fatty acids	0.3 g

Jump-Up-and-Down Fudgsicles

These look like cocoa-made Fudgsicles, and taste a lot like them, but surprise—they're made with carob.

Nutrisip: Carob is a healthier choice than chocolate because it doesn't contain caffeine or theobromine (an alkaloid similar to caffeine) as do cocoa or chocolate. Also, it contains protein, calcium, phosphorus, and some B vitamins.

1 cup soy milk or milk of choice
2 tablespoons carob powder
1 teaspoon pure vanilla extract
1 frozen or fresh banana, cut in chunks

Pour the milk into a blender and add the carob, vanilla, and banana. Blend on high speed until smooth, pour the mixture into six 3-ounce popsicle molds, and freeze.

Healthy-Pregnancy Smoothies and New-Parent Pick-Me-Uppers

Getting the best nutrition before and during pregnancy can have long-lasting positive effects for you and your baby; optimal nutrients influence fetal development and contribute to an uncomplicated delivery. Sadly, surveys show that significant numbers of American women of childbearing age consume diets that are low in nutrients associated with a healthy pregnancy, such as folic acid, vitamin B6, calcium, iron, and zinc. The smoothies in this book can help you increase these nutrients in yummy blends that are easy to digest and fast to make.

You may have some challenges during pregnancy such as morning sickness or constipation. The Morning-Sickness Mender (page 235) contains gingerroot, which has been shown in studies to help decrease vomiting and nausea associated with morning sickness. For constipation, fiber-rich foods should be increased, such as fruits, vegetables, and whole grains. Also, drink at least eight glasses of water daily, and eat dried fruits such as prunes. Try the Colon Care smoothie that incorporates prunes (page 137). Iron deficiency is common during pregnancy; iron demands increase during the second and third trimesters of pregnancy. Make more smoothies with iron-rich foods such as parsley, spinach, cashews, almonds, prunes, dates, strawberries, raisins, blackberries, and bananas.

After your baby is born, optimum nutrition for healthy breastfeeding is as important as eating right during pregnancy. The nutrients your baby could not or did not store during pregnancy must be obtained from breast milk. Once again, smoothies can be an important component of your diet that supplies some of the most important nutrients, such as vitamin B6, vitamin D, calcium, iron, and zinc. Also, you might try some of the tomato-based smoothies in other sections and add a clove of garlic. One study found that garlic enhanced breast milk; babies liked it, as evidenced by their sucking longer and consuming more milk. Be sure to try Mom's Iced Milk Flow (page 247) as well.

And for all the challenges you face as new parents, some of the smoothies in this section may help you relax by feeding your body the nutrients it requires to deal with all the stresses of having a new baby. For insomnia, try Sleepless-Night Smoothie (page 243), Arabian Nights and Sweet Dreams (page 141), or the New-Parents Serenity Sipper (page 245). And when your baby is ready for his or her first solid food, a smoothie such as Baby's First Smoothie (page 251) is a must, along with Baby's Teething Popsicle (page 253).

Morning-Sickness Mender

Total Weight:	19.0 oz.	Serving Size:	9.5 oz.

Serves 2

BASIC COMPONENTS			
Calories	88.8	Folate	2.3 mcg
Calories from fat	0.1	MINERALS	
Protein	0.1 g	Calcium	3.1 mg
Carbohydrates	22.5 g	Iron	0.0 mg
Dietary fiber	0.1 g	Magnesium	2.3 mg
Sugar—total	21.5 g	Potassium	252.5 mg
Fat—total	0.0 g	Selenium	0.0 mcg
Saturated fat	0.0 g	Sodium	23.3 mg
Monounsaturated fat	0.0 g	Zinc	0.0 mg
Polyunsaturated fat	0.0 g	OTHER FATS	
VITAMINS		Omega-3 fatty acids	0.0 g
A—beta-carotene	6.9 mcg	Omega-6 fatty acids	0.0 g
Vitamin B6	0.0 mg		
Vitamin C	7.1 mg		
Vitamin E	0.0 IU		

Morning-Sickness Mender

This shake has a very thin, juicy consistency, which helps when you can't keep much in your stomach.

Nutrisip: Gingerroot is known to help relieve the nausea and vomiting of morning sickness. Mint is an ancient remedy used to aid digestion. And apples have long been hailed as tummy soothers.

*1 1/2 cups apple juice (3 apples, juiced)**
1/2 lemon, juiced, peeled if using a juice machine
1- to 2-inch chunk gingerroot, juiced or grated
8 fresh mint leaves, rinsed
6 ice cubes

Pour the apple, lemon, and ginger juices (or grated ginger) into a blender and add the mint and ice. Blend on high speed until smooth and serve immediately.

**If you don't have a juice machine, and you are using commercial apple juice, get unsweetened and hand-squeeze the lemon, then grate the gingerroot and add to the blender.*

Super Calcium Booster

Total Weight: 13.6 oz. Serving Size: 6.8 oz.

Serves 2

Basic Components

Calories	105.9
Calories from fat	14.0
Protein	4.0 g
Carbohydrates	21.0 g
Dietary fiber	1.7 g
Sugar—total	17.6 g
Fat—total	1.6 g
Saturated fat	0.7 g
Monounsaturated fat	0.3 g
Polyunsaturated fat	0.2 g
Vitamins	
A—beta-carotene	125.6 mcg
Vitamin B6	0.2 mg
Vitamin C	21.8 mg
Vitamin E	0.3 IU
Folate	21.3 mcg
Minerals	
Calcium	125.1 mg
Iron	0.6 mg
Magnesium	33.1 mg
Potassium	335.7 mg
Selenium	2.8 mcg
Sodium	46.6 mg
Zinc	0.7 mg
Other Fats	
Omega-3 fatty acids	0.1 g
Omega-6 fatty acids	0.1 g

Super Calcium Booster

This is such a delicious smoothie, you'll hardly believe it has kale in it.

Nutrisip: Kale is called King Kale for a reason—it's one of nature's best sources of calcium and folic acid. Calcium requirements increase during pregnancy. Between 50 and 350 milligrams of calcium is transferred daily from the mother's blood to the baby. If dietary calcium is not sufficient to meet those needs, calcium is taken from the mother's bones. Calcium-rich smoothies can help you each day to meet your 1,200 milligrams of this important mineral.

1/2 pineapple, peeled and cut into chunks; save the core to juice
*1 kale leaf, rinsed and juiced**
1/2- to 1-inch gingerroot, juiced
1/2 cup plain low-fat yogurt
6 ice cubes

Juice the pineapple core with the kale and ginger. Pour the juice into a blender with the yogurt, and add the pineapple chunks and ice. Blend on high speed until smooth and serve immediately.

**If you don't have a juice machine, chop the kale in small pieces and grate the gingerroot.*

Mommy-To-Be Folic-Acid Special

Total Weight: 16.6 oz. Serving Size: 8.3 oz.

Serves 2

Basic Components

Calories	193.6
Calories from fat	56.1
Protein	9.3 g
Carbohydrates	26.3 g
Dietary fiber	3.5 g
Sugar—total	20.7 g
Fat—total	6.2 g
Saturated fat	2.1 g
Monounsaturated fat	2.5 g
Polyunsaturated fat	1.3 g
Vitamins	
A—beta-carotene	24.8 mcg
Vitamin B6	0.1 mg
Vitamin C	509.3 mg
Vitamin E	1.7 IU
Folate	32.3 mcg
Minerals	
Calcium	243.7 mg
Iron	0.8 mg
Magnesium	43.2 mg
Potassium	478.9 mg
Selenium	5.1 mcg
Sodium	124.8 mg
Zinc	1.5 mg
Other Fats	
Omega-3 fatty acids	0.1 g
Omega-6 fatty acids	1.2 g

Mommy-to-Be Folic-Acid Special

This has a nice thick consistency and fabulous flavor.

Nutrisip: Studies have now proved that folic acid helps prevent neural tube defects such as spina bifida (open spine) and anencephaly (lack of spine). These birth defects occur in the first 28 days after conception; therefore, it's important to get 400 milligrams of folic acid daily. Ample folic acid intake also decreases the risk for preterm delivery and low-birthweight infants. Wheat germ, peanut butter, and blackberries are good sources of folic acid.

1 cup plain low-fat yogurt
1/2 cup fresh or frozen blackberries, rinsed if fresh
1/2 cup unsweetened applesauce
1 tablespoon peanut butter, creamy or crunchy
1 tablespoon wheat germ
1 teaspoon pure vanilla extract
1 teaspoon honey
1/2 teaspoon ascorbic acid (vitamin C powder)

Combine the yogurt in a blender with the blackberries, applesauce, peanut butter, wheat germ, vanilla, honey and ascorbic acid. Blend on high speed until smooth and serve immediately.

Folic acid is such an important nutrient to consume while you are pregnant that a list of foods rich in this B vitamin should be close at hand. Some of your best sources of folic acid in the order of concentration are:

brewer's yeast
wheat germ
soy foods
bran
beans
asparagus
lentils
walnuts
spinach
kale
peanuts
broccoli
barley
split peas
whole wheat
Brussels sprouts
almonds
oatmeal
cabbage
figs
avocado
green beans
corn
dates
blackberries
oranges

Expectant Mom's Childbirth Helper

Total Weight:	13.2 oz.	Serving Size:	6.6 oz.

Serves 2

Basic Components

Calories	73.6
Calories from fat	1.1
Protein	0.8 g
Carbohydrates	18.0 g
Dietary fiber	1.3 g
Sugar—total	16.5 g
Fat—total	0.1 g
Saturated fat	0.0 g
Monounsaturated fat	0.0 g
Polyunsaturated fat	0.1 g
Vitamins	
A—beta-carotene	166.3 mcg
Vitamin B6	0.0 mg
Vitamin C	27.5 mg
Vitamin E	0.7 IU
Folate	10.8 mcg
Minerals	
Calcium	9.9 mg
Iron	0.2 mg
Magnesium	13.0 mg
Potassium	233.0 mg
Selenium	0.4 mcg
Sodium	2.6 mg
Zinc	0.1 mg
Other Fats	
Omega-3 fatty acids	0.0 g
Omega-6 fatty acids	0.0 g

Expectant Mom's Childbirth Helper

A pretty peachy color with a burst of raspberry flavor.

Nutrisip: Raspberry leaf tea is said to tone the uterine and pelvic muscles. It has been noted by one doctor that "in a great many cases labor has been free and easy from muscular spasms." Raspberry leaf tea can be taken during the last three months of pregnancy. This tea also is known to enrich and stimulate the flow of mother's milk.

6 Raspberry Zinger herbal tea ice cubes
1/2 cup white grape juice (1 cup green grapes, juiced)
1 large ripe peach, washed, pitted, and sliced (about 1 cup slices) or 1 cup frozen peaches
1/4 teaspoon pure raspberry extract

Steep one bag of Raspberry Zinger tea in a cup of hot water for about 20 minutes or until the tea is strong and flavorful. Pour into six ice cube tray squares and freeze. Pour the grape juice into a blender and add the peach slices and raspberry extract. Top with the raspberry ice cubes. Blend on high speed until smooth and serve immediately.

Sleepless-Night Smoothie

Total Weight: 15.0 oz. Serving Size: 7.5 oz.

Serves 2

Basic Components

Calories	181.4
Calories from fat	90.6
Protein	5.2 g
Carbohydrates	18.7 g
Dietary fiber	1.0 g
Sugar—total	14.8 g
Fat—total	10.1 g
Saturated fat	2.4 g
Monounsaturated fat	3.6 g
Polyunsaturated fat	3.6 g

Vitamins

A—beta-carotene	38.1 mcg
Vitamin B6	0.1 mg
Vitamin C	33.4 mg
Vitamin E	0.7 IU
Folate	39.1 mcg

Minerals

Calcium	105.6 mg
Iron	0.9 mg
Magnesium	29.4 mg
Potassium	295.1 mg
Selenium	1.7 mcg
Sodium	36.8 mg
Zinc	1.1 mg

Other Fats

Omega-3 fatty acids	0.0 g
Omega-6 fatty acids	0.1 g

Sleepless-Night Smoothie

Makes enough for Daddy, too, so he can sleep.

Nutrisip: Yogurt is a good source of tryptophan, the main amino acid that helps induce sleep. It is a precursor to melatonin, the body's primary sleep hormone. Chlorella and blue-green algae are also sources of tryptophan. Yogurt, tahini, and oranges are good sources of calcium, which helps muscles relax.

1/2 cup orange juice (1–2 oranges, juiced, peeled if using a juice machine)
1/2 cup plain low-fat yogurt
2 tablespoons tahini (sesame butter)
2 teaspoons honey
1 teaspoon pure vanilla extract
1 teaspoon freshly grated orange peel, preferably organic
1 teaspoon chlorella or blue-green algae (optional)
6 ice cubes

Pour the orange juice into a blender and add the yogurt, tahini, honey, vanilla, orange peel, chlorella or algae as desired, and ice. Blend on high speed until smooth and serve immediately.

New-Parents Serenity Sipper

Total Weight:	15.0 oz.	Serving Size:	7.5 oz.

Serves 2

Basic Components

Calories	142.0	Vitamin E	0.5 IU
Calories from fat	82.4	Folate	17.0 mcg
Protein	4.4 g	Minerals	
Carbohydrates	12.0 g	Calcium	27.9 mg
Dietary fiber	2.3 g	Iron	1.1 mg
Sugar—total	6.4 g	Magnesium	28.9 mg
Fat—total	9.2 g	Potassium	211.2 mg
Saturated fat	1.3 g	Selenium	1.3 mcg
Monounsaturated fat	3.2 g	Sodium	15.9 mg
Polyunsaturated fat	4.0 g	Zinc	0.9 mg
Vitamins		Other Fats	
A—beta-carotene	8.5 mcg	Omega-3 fatty acids	0.1 g
Vitamin B6	0.1 mg	Omega-6 fatty acids	0.5 g
Vitamin C	5.5 mg		

New-Parents Serenity Sipper

Everyone will like this smoothie—mommies, daddies, and siblings, too. It tastes like lemon cheesecake.

Nutrisip: The physical stress of sleepless nights and constant demands can deplete your body of valuable nutrients. Load up with calcium, iron, and vitamin C from this smoothie. Soy and tahini are rich in calcium, a nutrient that is important in helping you to relax and sleep through the night without waking up (unless a little someone wakes you up). Lemon has vitamin C to support your immune system, and iron from the tahini will help improve your energy level.

1/2 cup plain soy milk or milk of choice
1/2 cup unsweetened applesauce
2 tablespoons tahini (sesame butter)
1 tablespoon fresh lemon juice
1 teaspoon pure vanilla extract
1/2–1 teaspoon freshly grated lemon peel, preferably organic
6 ice cubes

Pour the milk into a blender and add the applesauce, tahini, lemon juice, vanilla, lemon peel, and ice. Blend on high speed until smooth and serve immediately.

Mom's Iced Milk Flow

Total Weight:	11.3 oz.	Serving Size:	11.3 oz.

Serves 1

Basic Components

Calories	280.0	Vitamin E	2.9 IU
Calories from fat	80.8	Folate	50.2 mcg
Protein	6.1 g	**Minerals**	
Carbohydrates	49.4 g	Calcium	45.6 mg
Dietary fiber	5.6 g	Iron	1.2 mg
Sugar—total	36.8 g	Magnesium	74.1 mg
Fat—total	9.0 g	Potassium	935.9 mg
Saturated fat	1.9 g	Selenium	2.9 mcg
Monounsaturated fat	3.9 g	Sodium	107.6 mg
Polyunsaturated fat	2.3 g	Zinc	0.8 mg
Vitamins		**Other Fats**	
A—beta-carotene	102.3 mcg	Omega-3 fatty acids	0.1 g
Vitamin B6	0.8 mg	Omega-6 fatty acids	2.3 g
Vitamin C	303.2 mg		

Mom's Iced Milk Flow

Bet you'll ask, "How could anything this good for you taste this great?"

Nutrisip: Fennel has been used since ancient times to help promote the flow of breast milk.

- *1/2 cup apple juice (1 medium apple, juiced)*
- *1/4 cup fresh fennel juice (about 1/4 medium bulb with feathery shoots)**
- *1 tablespoon peanut butter, crunchy or creamy*
- *1/4 teaspoon ascorbic acid (vitamin C powder)*
- *1 frozen banana, cut in chunks*

Pour the apple and fennel juices into a blender and add the peanut butter, ascorbic acid, and banana. Blend on high speed until smooth and serve immediately.

**If you don't have a juice machine, chop the fennel into small pieces; add 1/2 cup chopped fennel.*

Banana Almond Flip

Total Weight:	15.8 oz.	Serving Size:	15.8 oz.

Serves 1

BASIC COMPONENTS

Calories	609.3
Calories from fat	350.0
Protein	19.6 g
Carbohydrates	48.8 g
Dietary fiber	13.8 g
Sugar—total	30.5 g
Fat—total	38.9 g
Saturated fat	0.5 g
Monounsaturated fat	0.5 g
Polyunsaturated fat	1.1 g
VITAMINS	
A—beta-carotene	56.7 mcg
Vitamin B6	0.8 mg
Vitamin C	10.8 mg
Vitamin E	22.4 IU
Folate	51.5 mcg
MINERALS	
Calcium	198.4 mg
Iron	3.8 mg
Magnesium	273.6 mg
Potassium	1077.3 mg
Selenium	3.0 mcg
Sodium	20.0 mg
Zinc	2.9 mg
OTHER FATS	
Omega-3 fatty acids	0.2 g
Omega-6 fatty acids	1.0 g

Banana Almond Flip

Soothing and a great comfort food.

Nutrisip: Bananas are a good source of vitamin B6, which is an especially important nutrient for lactating women. Requirements for this vitamin go up during breastfeeding. One study found that Apgar scores were higher for infants of mothers who consumed several times the B6 RDA than for those of mothers who took in close to the RDA. (Apgar scores on infants are predictors of general health and well-being.)

1/2 cup plain soy milk or milk of choice
1/2 cup raw almonds
1 teaspoon honey or pure maple syrup
1/8 teaspoon pure almond extract
1 banana, peeled and cut into chunks
6 ice cubes
Pinch of nutmeg

Pour the soy milk into a blender and add the almonds, sweetener, almond extract, banana, and ice; top with the pinch of nutmeg. Blend on high speed until smooth and serve immediately.

Baby's First Smoothie

Total Weight:	12.8 oz.	Serving Size:	12.8 oz.

Serves 1

BASIC COMPONENTS			
Calories	200.2	Vitamin E	1.4 IU
Calories from fat	28.7	Folate	34.1 mcg
Protein	5.2 g	MINERALS	
Carbohydrates	42.9 g	Calcium	16.9 mg
Dietary fiber	8.8 g	Iron	1.1 mg
Sugar—total	30.7 g	Magnesium	67.3 mg
Fat—total	3.2 g	Potassium	787.6 mg
Saturated fat	0.5 g	Selenium	3.6 mcg
Monounsaturated fat	0.5 g	Sodium	15.9 mg
Polyunsaturated fat	1.2 g	Zinc	0.5 mg
VITAMINS		OTHER FATS	
A—beta-carotene	56.6 mcg	Omega-3 fatty acids	0.2 g
Vitamin B6	0.8 mg	Omega-6 fatty acids	1.0 g
Vitamin C	15.4 mg		

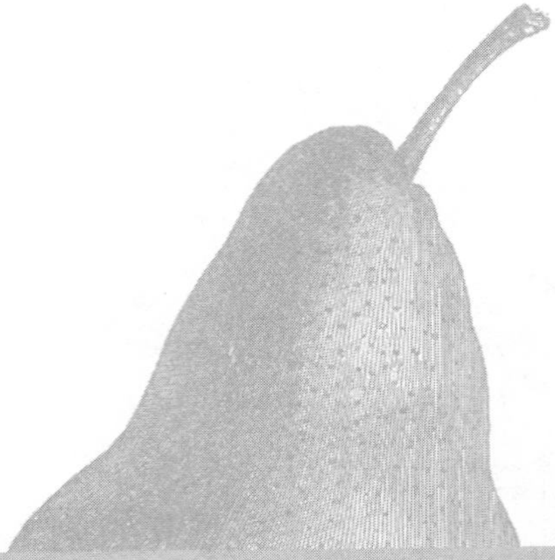

Baby's First Smoothie

This shake tastes like baby food, so your baby should like it! Best of all, it's fresh and has not undergone processing, which kills nutrients. It's also free of additives.

Nutrisip: Mild fruits such as pear, banana, and peach are recommended for the first fruits your baby eats. Watch apple juice; it can cause diarrhea in some children.

1/2 cup soy milk or milk of choice
1 banana, peeled and cut into chunks
1 ripe pear, peeled, cored, and cut into chunks

Pour the milk into a blender and add the banana and pear. Blend on high speed until smooth. Serve immediately or store covered in the refrigerator until ready to serve.

Baby's Teething Popsicle

Total Weight: 16.0 oz. Serving Size: 2.0 oz.

Makes 8

BASIC COMPONENTS

Calories	33.2
Calories from fat	2.9
Protein	0.4 g
Carbohydrates	8.1 g
Dietary fiber	1.2 g
Sugar—total	4.9 g
Fat—total	0.3 g
Saturated fat	0.0 g
Monounsaturated fat	0.0 g
Polyunsaturated fat	0.0 g
VITAMINS	
A—beta-carotene	48.5 mcg
Vitamin B6	0.1 mg
Vitamin C	4.3 mg
Vitamin E	0.1 IU
Folate	2.6 mcg
MINERALS	
Calcium	1.1 mg
Iron	0.0 mg
Magnesium	3.4 mg
Potassium	102.7 mg
Selenium	0.2 mcg
Sodium	0.1 mg
Zinc	0.0 mg
OTHER FATS	
Omega-3 fatty acids	0.0 g
Omega-6 fatty acids	0.0 g

Baby's Teething Popsicle

A yummy popsicle for sore gums.

Nutrisip: When your baby is screaming with the pain of new teeth, try a cold popsicle to help relieve the pain, and delicious flavor to heal the soul.

4 small purple plums (Italian prune plums), washed, cut in half, seeds removed, or 1 cup sliced peaches, fresh or frozen
1 pear, stem removed, washed, peeled and cut into chunks
1/2 banana, peeled and cut into chunks

Combine the plums or peaches, pear, and banana in a blender and blend on high speed until smooth. Pour the mixture into eight popsicle molds and freeze until ready to use.

Exotic Smoothies and Shakes

Many ethnic beverages have for centuries included yogurt, fruit, nuts, seeds, and herbs to make enzyme-rich, health-promoting drinks that accompany meals. Worldwide, these drinks have been valued for their ability to relieve indigestion and constipation, promote lactation, invigorate the weak, strengthen the sick, and promote stamina and well-being.

I have included a number of *lassis* in this section—traditional beverages served in India that use yogurt as a base blended with fruit and spices. Lassis are also used in Ayurvedic cooking, which is the Indian system of healing. Lassis are cooling when served with hot foods such as curries and are refreshing on a hot summer day. Lassis also make great snacks or quick meals. Traditionally, they do not have ice blended with them.

The beverages in this section can revitalize a tired body by supplying minerals depleted through perspiration, while at the same time they facilitate easy and thorough assimilation of food with their lactobacilli and enzymes.

Strawberry Rosewater Lassi

Total Weight:	13.6 oz.	Serving Size:	6.8 oz.

Serves 2

BASIC COMPONENTS

Calories	117.6
Calories from fat	19.1
Protein	6.8 g
Carbohydrates	18.9 g
Dietary fiber	1.4 g
Sugar—total	17.1 g
Fat—total	2.1 g
Saturated fat	1.2 g
Monounsaturated fat	0.6 g
Polyunsaturated fat	0.2 g

VITAMINS

A—beta-carotene	10.0 mcg
Vitamin B6	0.1 mg
Vitamin C	36.2 mg
Vitamin E	0.2 IU
Folate	24.8 mcg

MINERALS

Calcium	232.7 mg
Iron	0.4 mg
Magnesium	27.7 mg
Potassium	392.8 mg
Selenium	4.5 mcg
Sodium	86.9 mg
Zinc	1.2 mg

OTHER FATS

Omega-3 fatty acids	0.1 g
Omega-6 fatty acids	0.1 g

Strawberry Rosewater Lassi

Rosewater can be purchased at Middle Eastern stores, specialty cooking shops, and some health food stores. It's worth looking for, as it adds a delicate floral flavor to shakes and smoothies.

Nutrisip: Here's a nutrition question for you: Which has more vitamin C—strawberries or oranges? Answer: the berries.

1 cup plain low-fat yogurt
10 strawberries, washed, caps removed
2 teaspoons honey
1 teaspoon rosewater
6 ice cubes (optional)

Combine the yogurt, strawberries, honey, rosewater, and ice as desired in a blender and process until smooth. Serve immediately. (Ice cubes are optional because in Ayurvedic cooking, beverages are served at room temperature to aid digestion. Cold drinks are considered too taxing to the digestive system.)

Orange Blossom

Total Weight:	13.4 oz.	Serving Size:	6.7 oz.

Serves 2

Basic Components

Calories	96.2
Calories from fat	10.8
Protein	4.1 g
Carbohydrates	17.7 g
Dietary fiber	0.4 g
Sugar—total	17.1 g
Fat—total	1.2 g
Saturated fat	0.6 g
Monounsaturated fat	0.3 g
Polyunsaturated fat	0.1 g

Vitamins

A—beta-carotene	49.0 mcg
Vitamin B6	0.1 mg
Vitamin C	65.0 mg
Vitamin E	0.2 IU
Folate	45.1 mcg

Minerals

Calcium	127.3 mg
Iron	0.3 mg
Magnesium	24.7 mg
Potassium	396.5 mg
Selenium	2.2 mcg
Sodium	44.3 mg
Zinc	0.6 mg

Other Fats

Omega-3 fatty acids	0.0 g
Omega-6 fatty acids	0.1 g

Orange Blossom

A tart and refreshing drink! Orange blossom water can be purchased at Middle Eastern stores, specialty cooking shops, and some health food stores.

Nutrisip: When you juice an orange, cut the outer peel off because it contains oils that are bitter and too strong in large quantity for the stomach. But leave as much of the white pithy part on the orange as possible because that contains the most vitamin C and bioflavonoids.

1 cup orange juice (2 medium oranges, juiced, peeled if using a juice machine)
1/2 cup plain low-fat yogurt
1 teaspoon orange blossom water
1 teaspoon grated orange peel, preferably organic
6 ice cubes (optional)

Pour the orange juice into a blender and add the yogurt, orange blossom water, orange peel, and ice cubes as desired. Blend on high speed until smooth and serve immediately. (Ice cubes are optional because in Ayurvedic cooking, beverages are served at room temperature to aid digestion; this drink would be considered a lassi. Cold drinks are considered too taxing to the digestive system.)

Honey Mint Tulip

Total Weight:	14.2 oz.	Serving Size:	7.1 oz.

Serves 2

BASIC COMPONENTS

Calories	110.5
Calories from fat	17.2
Protein	6.5 g
Carbohydrates	17.5 g
Dietary fiber	0.0 g
Sugar—total	16.9 g
Fat—total	1.9 g
Saturated fat	1.2 g
Monounsaturated fat	0.5 g
Polyunsaturated fat	0.1 g

VITAMINS

A—beta-carotene	4.5 mcg
Vitamin B6	0.1 mg
Vitamin C	1.1 mg
Vitamin E	0.2 IU
Folate	14.5 mcg

MINERALS

Calcium	226.1 mg
Iron	0.2 mg
Magnesium	22.4 mg
Potassium	298.9 mg
Selenium	4.1 mcg
Sodium	87.1 mg
Zinc	1.1 mg

OTHER FATS

Omega-3 fatty acids	0.0 g
Omega-6 fatty acids	0.0 g

Honey Mint Tulip

Mint is used in Ayurvedic cooking for its cooling properties. This would be a good beverage to serve with a hot, spicy meal.

Nutrisip: Mint is very good for digestion, demonstrating an antispasmodic effect on the smooth muscles of the digestive tract.

6 peppermint herbal tea ice cubes
1 cup plain low-fat yogurt
1 tablespoon honey
6–8 fresh mint leaves, rinsed

Steep one peppermint herbal tea bag in a cup of hot water for about 20 minutes, or until the tea is strong and flavorful. Pour the tea into six ice cube tray squares and freeze. Combine the yogurt in a blender with the honey, mint leaves, and peppermint ice cubes. Blend on high speed until smooth and serve immediately.

Mango Lassi

Total Weight:	16.4 oz.	Serving Size:	8.2 oz.

Serves 2

Basic Components

Calories	160.9
Calories from fat	19.6
Protein	7.0 g
Carbohydrates	30.6 g
Dietary fiber	1.9 g
Sugar—total	28.1 g
Fat—total	2.2 g
Saturated fat	1.3 g
Monounsaturated fat	0.6 g
Polyunsaturated fat	0.1 g

Vitamins

A—beta-carotene	2415.7 mcg
Vitamin B6	0.2 mg
Vitamin C	29.7 mg
Vitamin E	1.8 IU
Folate	28.3 mcg

Minerals

Calcium	234.4 mg
Iron	0.3 mg
Magnesium	30.8 mg
Potassium	450.6 mg
Selenium	4.7 mcg
Sodium	88.3 mg
Zinc	1.1 mg

Other Fats

Omega-3 fatty acids	0.1 g
Omega-6 fatty acids	0.1 g

Mango Lassi

Mango lassis are served in many Indian restaurants in North America but are typically much sweeter than this version. If you prefer a very sweet mango lassi, add more honey.

Nutrisip: Mangoes are a good source of beta-carotene, vitamin C, and potassium, and therefore a nutritious choice, if grown in the United States. Those coming from other countries can be sprayed with chemicals banned in the U.S.

1 cup plain low-fat yogurt
1 medium mango, peeled and cut into chunks from the pit
1–2 teaspoons honey
6 ice cubes (optional)

Combine the yogurt in a blender with the mango, honey, and ice cubes as desired. Blend on high speed until smooth and serve immediately. (Ice cubes are optional because in Ayurvedic cooking, beverages are served at room temperature to aid digestion. Cold drinks are considered too taxing to the digestive system.)

Cantaloupe Frosty

Total Weight:	14.6 oz.	Serving Size:	7.3 oz.

Serves 2

Basic Components

Calories	46.0	Vitamin E	0.3 IU
Calories from fat	3.3	Folate	22.3 mcg
Protein	1.2 g	**Minerals**	
Carbohydrates	11.0 g	Calcium	15.7 mg
Dietary fiber	1.1 g	Iron	0.3 mg
Sugar—total	10.0 g	Magnesium	15.1 mg
Fat—total	0.4 g	Potassium	406.1 mg
Saturated fat	0.1 g	Selenium	0.5 mcg
Monounsaturated fat	0.0 g	Sodium	13.7 mg
Polyunsaturated fat	0.1 g	Zinc	0.2 mg
Vitamins		**Other Fats**	
A—beta-carotene	2523.4 mcg	Omega-3 fatty acids	0.1 g
Vitamin B6	0.2 mg	Omega-6 fatty acids	0.1 g
Vitamin C	55.5 mg		

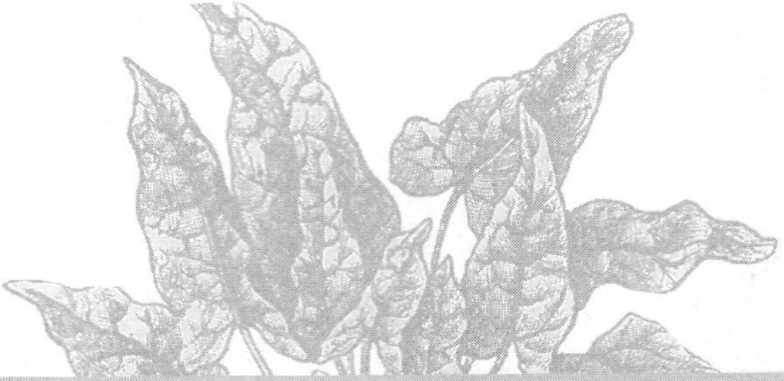

Cantaloupe Frosty

Refreshing on a warm day, this beautiful pastel peach-colored drink blends frozen tea with sweet cantaloupe for a delicate mix of flavors. This is a great way to use leftover tea.

Nutrisip: Cantaloupe is a good source of inositol, a vitamin that is needed for proper brain, nerve, and muscle function.

6 lemon grass, green tea, or mint tea ice cubes

1/2 cantaloupe, peeled and cut into chunks

Steep one bag of tea in hot water for about 20 minutes; pour into six ice cube tray squares and freeze. (This is a great use for leftover tea.) Combine the tea ice cubes and cantaloupe in a blender on high speed until smooth. Serve immediately.

Sweet Bliss

Total Weight: 24.8 oz. Serving Size: 12.4 oz.

Serves 2

BASIC COMPONENTS

Calories	203.1
Calories from fat	11.4
Protein	4.0 g
Carbohydrates	44.7 g
Dietary fiber	3.4 g
Sugar—total	41.2 g
Fat—total	1.3 g
Saturated fat	0.7 g
Monounsaturated fat	0.3 g
Polyunsaturated fat	0.2 g

VITAMINS

A—beta-carotene	84.2 mcg
Vitamin B6	0.1 mg
Vitamin C	2.5 mg
Vitamin E	1.4 IU
Folate	12.9 mcg

MINERALS

Calcium	148.3 mg
Iron	0.4 mg
Magnesium	27.7 mg
Potassium	602.5 mg
Selenium	2.6 mcg
Sodium	65.7 mg
Zinc	0.7 mg

OTHER FATS

Omega-3 fatty acids	0.0 g
Omega-6 fatty acids	0.2 g

Sweet Bliss

This mix of spices and fruit has a Middle Eastern flavor.

Nutrisip: Apples are rich in pectin, water-soluble fiber, which slows the absorption of food after meals, making it good for diabetics and helpful for everyone's colon. When you make your own apple juice, you can make sure you're using the skin, which contains the most pectin. Organically grown is the best choice to avoid chemicals and waxes. If organic is not available, then peel the apples.

1 1/2 cups apple juice (about 3 apples juiced)
1/2 cup plain low-fat yogurt
5 small fresh ripe black figs, cut in half (dried figs can be used but must first be soaked to soften)
1/2 teaspoon pure almond extract
1/4 teaspoon ground cloves

Pour the apple juice into a blender and add the yogurt, figs, almond extract, and cloves. Blend on high speed until smooth and serve immediately.

Pineapple Mint

Total Weight: 16.8 oz. Serving Size: 8.4 oz.

Serves 2

BASIC COMPONENTS

Calories	118.8
Calories from fat	14.5
Protein	3.1 g
Carbohydrates	22.3 g
Dietary fiber	0.2 g
Sugar—total	17.5 g
Fat—total	1.6 g
Saturated fat	0.2 g
Monounsaturated fat	0.3 g
Polyunsaturated fat	0.9 g

VITAMINS

A—beta-carotene	70.1 mcg
Vitamin B6	0.0 mg
Vitamin C	57.8 mg
Vitamin E	0.3 IU
Folate	14.8 mcg

MINERALS

Calcium	23.8 mg
Iron	0.6 mg
Magnesium	22.1 mg
Potassium	360.1 mg
Selenium	0.1 mcg
Sodium	8.5 mg
Zinc	0.3 mg

OTHER FATS

Omega-3 fatty acids	0.0 g
Omega-6 fatty acids	0.0 g

Pineapple Mint

You could consider this drink a vegan lassi, since it is made with tofu instead of dairy yogurt.

Nutrisip: Bromelain, a protein-digesting enzyme found in pineapple, helps aid the digestion of protein. Mint is cooling and also promotes good digestion, making this beverage quite beneficial with meals.

1 cup pineapple juice (juice about 1/2 medium-size ripe pineapple; remove the skin before juicing; juice the core)
1/3 cup orange juice (about 1/2 orange juiced, peel removed)
2 tablespoons fresh lemon juice
4 ounces soft silken tofu
10 fresh mint leaves, rinsed

Pour the pineapple, orange, and lemon juices into a blender and add the tofu and mint. Blend on high speed until smooth and serve immediately.

Luncheon Smoothies and Cold Soups

Soups, cold or hot, are much more than a starter for meals. They can refresh your body and soul on a warm day or be a healing tonic when you're ill. In many cultures worldwide, soup has been used therapeutically. For example, in India, certain soups are used to tone up the stomach and nervous system.

The luncheon smoothies and cold soups in this section take only a few minutes to make, and they can be a nutritious answer to eating healthfully on busy days. Soups are also recommended for those who want to lose weight, because we tend to eat them more slowly than other foods, sipping or spooning small bites at a time. Eating slowly can help our message center of the brain send the signal that we've satisfied our hunger needs before we've totally stuffed ourselves.

Smoothie soups may be a new idea for you, because we typically think of smoothies as sweet concoctions that look and taste like ice cream milk shakes. But they can be equally appealing as savory meals-in-a-glass. Take Vicki's Tangy Tomato (page 277), for example; it's very refreshing and actually all you'll need for lunch, except for maybe a few crackers or some vegetable sticks. The Roasted Red Pepper Soup (page 281) tastes something like a soup I had at a fine restaurant somewhere in the course of my many travels. I served it with homemade corn bread and that made a complete dinner meal.

I think you'll come to enjoy luncheon smoothies as much as the fruity blends.

Yummy Tomato Creme Cooler

Total Weight:	20.8 oz.	Serving Size:	10.4 oz.

Serves 2

Basic Components

Calories	140.1
Calories from fat	64.3
Protein	5.5 g
Carbohydrates	16.9 g
Dietary fiber	4.1 g
Sugar—total	10.1 g
Fat—total	7.1 g
Saturated fat	1.6 g
Monounsaturated fat	3.9 g
Polyunsaturated fat	1.0 g

Vitamins

A—beta-carotene	773.6 mcg
Vitamin B6	0.3 mg
Vitamin C	56.8 mg
Vitamin E	1.8 IU
Folate	56.5 mcg

Minerals

Calcium	130.9 mg
Iron	1.3 mg
Magnesium	44.8 mg
Potassium	785.7 mg
Selenium	2.9 mcg
Sodium	64.5 mg
Zinc	0.9 mg

Other Fats

Omega-3 fatty acids	0.1 g
Omega-6 fatty acids	0.9 g

Yummy Tomato Creme Cooler

This is a refreshing and filling cold soup that takes only a few minutes to make. If you want to serve it in the winter, and an icy soup isn't appealing, don't freeze the tomato chunks.

Nutrisip: Tomatoes contain large amounts of lycopene, a powerful antioxidant that is touted to be the cancer-preventative nutrient in tomatoes.

2 cups tomatoes, washed and chopped
1/2 cup avocado, peeled, seeded, and chopped
1/2 cup plain low-fat yogurt
1/2 teaspoon freshly grated lemon peel, preferably organic
1/2 teaspoon balsamic vinegar
1/2 lemon, juiced, peeled if using a juice machine
Dash of cayenne pepper (optional)

Place the tomato chunks in a freezer bag and freeze until solid. Combine the tomato chunks, avocado, yogurt, lemon peel, balsamic vinegar, lemon juice, and cayenne as desired in a blender. Blend on high speed until smooth and serve immediately.

Green Vichyssoise

Total Weight:	35.2 oz.	Serving Size:	17.6 oz.

Serves 2

Basic Components

Calories	181.7
Calories from fat	72.7
Protein	4.5 g
Carbohydrates	22.5 g
Dietary fiber	4.2 g
Sugar—total	0.5 g
Fat—total	8.1 g
Saturated fat	0.8 g
Monounsaturated fat	1.4 g
Polyunsaturated fat	5.2 g
Vitamins	
A—beta-carotene	274.7 mcg
Vitamin B6	0.1 mg
Vitamin C	41.9 mg
Vitamin E	0.5 IU
Folate	15.9 mcg
Minerals	
Calcium	60.2 mg
Iron	1.8 mg
Magnesium	20.7 mg
Potassium	402.0 mg
Selenium	0.9 mcg
Sodium	1543.2 mg
Zinc	0.3 mg
Other Fats	
Omega-3 fatty acids	3.8 g
Omega-6 fatty acids	1.4 g

Green Vichyssoise

A cold soup with a French name, this version is actually an American invention. Vichyssoise is typically cooked first, then chilled. This soup has a pretty avocado color and only the potatoes are cooked first. All the other ingredients are raw, which preserves the vitamins and enzymes.

Nutrisip: Potatoes are rich in potassium, a mineral that plays a significant role in alleviating hypertension.

6 new potatoes with skin, cut into chunks (about 3 1/2 cups cooked)
1 cup water
1 medium cucumber, juiced
2 stalks celery, juiced
1/4 cup parsley, coarsely chopped
2 tablespoons leek or yellow or white onion, minced
1/2 cup soy milk or milk of choice
1 tablespoon pure cold-pressed flaxseed oil (optional)
1 teaspoon dried dill weed
1/2 teaspoon celery salt
1/2 teaspoon sea salt
Garnish: chopped chives, croutons, or roasted sunflower seeds

Barely cover the potatoes with water and cook for 20 minutes or until they are soft. Watch them so they don't stick or burn; add a bit of water near the end of the cooking time as needed. Chill the potatoes before blending. Chill the cucumber and celery before juicing. Pour the cucumber and celery juices into a blender and add the potatoes, parsley, leek or onion, milk, flax oil as desired, dill, celery salt, and sea salt. Blend on high speed until smooth. Pour into bowls and garnish as desired. Serve immediately. This soup is better if not allowed to sit.

Vicki's Tangy Tomato

Total Weight:	26.6 oz.	Serving Size:	13.3 oz.

Serves 2

Basic Components			
Calories	86.7	Vitamin E	1.0 IU
Calories from fat	8.1	Folate	28.8 mcg
Protein	3.4 g	**Minerals**	
Carbohydrates	19.2 g	Calcium	63.4 mg
Dietary fiber	2.1 g	Iron	1.1 mg
Sugar—total	6.3 g	Magnesium	23.1 mg
Fat—total	0.9 g	Potassium	822.9 mg
Saturated fat	0.1 g	Selenium	1.0 mcg
Monounsaturated fat	0.1 g	Sodium	446.0 mg
Polyunsaturated fat	0.4 g	Zinc	0.2 mg
Vitamins		**Other Fats**	
A—beta-carotene	2550.3 mcg	Omega-3 fatty acids	0.0 g
Vitamin B6	0.2 mg	Omega-6 fatty acids	0.4 g
Vitamin C	42.5 mg		

Vicki's Tangy Tomato

This is about the best vegetable smoothie I've ever tasted, thanks to Vicki Chelf.

Nutrisip: Tomatoes are a source of tyramine, which is a precursor of tyrosine, an amino acid. Thyroid hormones are made from iodine and tyrosine; therefore, it follows that tomatoes are helpful in promoting healthy thyroid balance.

3 medium tomatoes, cut into chunks
1 1/2 cups fresh carrot juice (about 6 large carrots)
1 tablespoon balsamic vinegar or fresh lemon juice
2 teaspoons tamari or low-sodium soy sauce
1 garlic clove, peeled
Garnish: finely chopped cilantro or parsley

Place the tomato chunks in a freezer bag and freeze them until solid. Pour the carrot juice, balsamic vinegar or lemon juice, and tamari or soy sauce in a blender and add the tomato chunks and garlic; blend on high speed until smooth. Garnish as desired and serve immediately.

Garlicky Avocado

Total Weight:	29.0 oz.	Serving Size:	14.5 oz.

Serves 2

Basic Components

Calories	228.4	Vitamin E	0.7 IU
Calories from fat	141.4	Folate	23.3 mcg
Protein	11.2 g	**Minerals**	
Carbohydrates	16.0 g	Calcium	89.7 mg
Dietary fiber	9.3 g	Iron	2.3 mg
Sugar—total	1.8 g	Magnesium	43.3 mg
Fat—total	15.7 g	Potassium	1521.8 mg
Saturated fat	2.9 g	Selenium	0.3 mcg
Monounsaturated fat	0.7 g	Sodium	173.2 mg
Polyunsaturated fat	1.8 g	Zinc	0.8 mg
Vitamins		**Other Fats**	
A—beta-carotene	516.1 mcg	Omega-3 fatty acids	0.0 g
Vitamin B6	0.1 mg	Omega-6 fatty acids	0.0 g
Vitamin C	74.1 mg		

Garlicky Avocado

This savory smoothie can be a luncheon or dinner soup.

Nutrisip: Studies have shown garlic's smelly compound, allicin, to have a natural antibiotic effect. Even breathing garlic is therapeutic, as evidenced by one study titled "A Whiff of Garlic Keeps Cancer at Bay." The rodents in this study that had garlic ropes hanging in their cages had the least incidence of cancer.

1 1/4 cups fresh cucumber juice (about l large or 2 medium cucumbers, peeled if not organic)
2 stalks celery, juiced
1 small avocado, peeled, seeded, and cut into chunks
1 garlic clove, peeled
8 ounces soft silken tofu
1/2 cup parsley, coarsely chopped
2 teaspoons onion, minced
1 teaspoon dried dill weed

Pour the cucumber and celery juices into a blender and add the avocado, garlic, tofu, parsley, onion, and dill. Blend on high speed until smooth and serve immediately. This soup is not good if it sits.

Roasted Red Pepper Soup

Total Weight:	27.6 oz.	Serving Size:	13.8 oz.

Serves 2

Basic Components

Calories	129.1	Vitamin E	2.6 IU
Calories from fat	25.9	Folate	58.3 mcg
Protein	6.8 g	**Minerals**	
Carbohydrates	22.6 g	Calcium	49.1 mg
Dietary fiber	6.8 g	Iron	2.2 mg
Sugar—total	7.9 g	Magnesium	53.7 mg
Fat—total	2.9 g	Potassium	669.9 mg
Saturated fat	0.3 g	Selenium	3.7 mcg
Monounsaturated fat	0.4 g	Sodium	358.3 mg
Polyunsaturated fat	1.3 g	Zinc	0.7 mg
Vitamins		**Other Fats**	
A—beta-carotene	7631.2 mcg	Omega-3 fatty acids	0.2 g
Vitamin B6	0.8 mg	Omega-6 fatty acids	1.2 g
Vitamin C	470.5 mg		

Roasted Red Pepper Soup

This cold soup tastes delicious served with homemade corn bread.

Nutrisip: Bell peppers are one of our best sources of vitamin C, which is such an important nutrient for a healthy immune system.

3 large red bell peppers, roasted
6 garlic cloves, roasted, skins removed
1 cup soy milk or milk of choice
1 tablespoon balsamic vinegar
2 teaspoons tamari or low-sodium soy sauce
6 fresh basil leaves, rinsed
Garnish: chopped fresh basil (optional)

Roast the peppers and garlic. (See below for roasting instructions.) Cut the peppers into chunks. Pour the milk into a blender and add the peppers, garlic, balsamic vinegar, tamari or soy sauce, and basil. Blend on high speed until smooth. Pour into bowls and garnish with fresh basil, as desired. Serve immediately.

Roasting Red Bell Peppers

To roast red peppers, turn the oven to Broil. Prick the peppers with a fork and place them in an ovenproof pan under the broiler until the skins turn black, turning occasionally to char evenly on all sides. (They don't have to be completely black on every inch.) If you hear them popping, don't worry; that's normal. Remove the peppers from the oven and place them in a paper bag to cool, then peel them and discard the stem, ribs, and seeds.

Roasting Garlic Cloves

Turn the oven to Broil. Place the garlic in a small ovenproof pan and drizzle with a bit of olive oil. Pour a small amount of water (about 1/4 cup) into the bottom of the pan and place under the broiler, turning occasionally, for about 5 minutes, or until soft.

Creamy Avocado

Total Weight:	15.6 oz.	Serving Size:	7.8 oz.

Serves 2

Basic Components

Calories	196.9	Vitamin E	0.0 IU
Calories from fat	123.1	Folate	2.2 mcg
Protein	4.3 g	**Minerals**	
Carbohydrates	18.2 g	Calcium	6.3 mg
Dietary fiber	8.5 g	Iron	0.4 mg
Sugar—total	8.8 g	Magnesium	13.1 mg
Fat—total	13.7 g	Potassium	527.9 mg
Saturated fat	2.6 g	Selenium	0.9 mcg
Monounsaturated fat	0.2 g	Sodium	9.9 mg
Polyunsaturated fat	0.5 g	Zinc	0.2 mg
Vitamins		**Other Fats**	
A—beta-carotene	1.2 mcg	Omega-3 fatty acids	0.1 g
Vitamin B6	0.0 mg	Omega-6 fatty acids	0.5 g
Vitamin C	10.9 mg		

Creamy Avocado

This light lemon avocado soup is very refreshing.

Nutrisip: So many people tell me they won't eat an avocado because it has too much fat. Actually, the fat in an avocado is good fat—it includes essential fatty acids. These fats are good for the skin and hair and help prevent heart disease. Avocados are also a good source of vegetable protein.

1/2 cup plain soy milk or milk of choice
1 medium avocado, peeled and seeded
1 tablespoon fresh lemon juice
1 tablespoon honey
1 teaspoon pure vanilla extract
1 teaspoon freshly grated lemon peel, preferably organic
6 ice cubes

Pour the milk into a blender and add the avocado, lemon juice, honey, vanilla, lemon peel, and ice. Blend on high speed until smooth and serve immediately.

Cucumber Mint Creme

Total Weight:	18.0 oz.	Serving Size:	6.0 oz.

Serves 3

Basic Components

Calories	65.4	Vitamin E	0.2 IU
Calories from fat	12.7	Folate	25.7 mcg
Protein	5.0 g	Minerals	
Carbohydrates	8.7 g	Calcium	168.6 mg
Dietary fiber	0.8 g	Iron	0.3 mg
Sugar—total	6.0 g	Magnesium	25.8 mg
Fat—total	1.4 g	Potassium	336.1 mg
Saturated fat	0.9 g	Selenium	2.9 mcg
Monounsaturated fat	0.4 g	Sodium	444.1 mg
Polyunsaturated fat	0.1 g	Zinc	0.9 mg
Vitamins		Other Fats	
A—beta-carotene	57.3 mcg	Omega-3 fatty acids	0.0 g
Vitamin B6	0.1 mg	Omega-6 fatty acids	0.1 g
Vitamin C	4.8 mg		

Cucumber Mint Creme

This light soup has a lot of flavor and can help you feel as if you've had a rich meal without the high calories.

Nutrisip: Cucumbers are among nature's best diuretics and are helpful for any weight-loss program.

1 cup plain low-fat yogurt (soy yogurt can be substituted, but it has a stronger flavor)
2 cups cucumber, peeled and diced
1/4 cup scallions, chopped
1/2 teaspoon sea salt
6 mint leaves, rinsed
1 garlic clove, peeled and minced

Combine the yogurt with the cucumber, scallions, salt, mint, and garlic in a blender and process on high speed until smooth. Pour into bowls and serve immediately.

Shakes and Smoothies for Summer Afternoons and Parties

What do you choose to drink on a warm summer day when you're thirsty? Soda pop? Diet drinks? A sugary powdered drink mix? An ice-cream shake? Wouldn't you like to choose something that's really good for your body as well as your taste buds?

There are problems with the drinks named above. Sugar-sweetened soft drinks and powdered drink mixes contain large quantities of sugar; a 12-ounce can of sugar-sweetened pop, for example, contains an average of 8 to 11 teaspoons of refined sugar. Diet sodas and diet powdered drinks are sweetened with artificial sweeteners, and every artificial sweetener on the market has some disadvantages. Saccharin can increase the risk of developing bladder cancer. Aspartame (popularly known as NutraSweet or Equal) has been linked with cases of hives, headaches, eyesight problems, epileptic seizures, and possibly brain tumors. Everyone should avoid these sweeteners, but especially pregnant women and children. Ice-cream shakes are loaded with sugars and often with artificial flavors.

When we think of party drinks, we usually think of drink mixes and alcohol. Most party drinks are loaded with sugar. Total consumption of sweeteners, including refined sugar and corn syrup, was about 143 pounds per person a year in the last decade. Sugar contributes to tooth decay, weakened immune responses, adult-onset diabetes, cancer, hypoglycemia, and acne. Party smoothies and afternoon blends are one way you can cut down on sugar consumption and help your family and friends do the same. The drinks in this section, and in the whole book for that matter, are really yummy, and you can make them festive and fun with just a simple garnish like an orange slice. Have fun and stay healthy!

Perky Piña Colada

Total Weight:	23.4 oz.	Serving Size:	11.7 oz.

Serves 2

Basic Components

Calories	235.6
Calories from fat	83.2
Protein	3.6 g
Carbohydrates	38.8 g
Dietary fiber	6.2 g
Sugar—total	30.8 g
Fat—total	9.3 g
Saturated fat	6.7 g
Monounsaturated fat	0.6 g
Polyunsaturated fat	0.8 g

Vitamins

A—beta-carotene	44.4 mcg
Vitamin B6	0.5 mg
Vitamin C	24.0 mg
Vitamin E	0.7 IU
Folate	31.3 mcg

Minerals

Calcium	21.1 mg
Iron	1.6 mg
Magnesium	55.5 mg
Potassium	582.6 mg
Selenium	4.5 mcg
Sodium	15.6 mg
Zinc	0.6 mg

Other Fats

Omega-3 fatty acids	0.2 g
Omega-6 fatty acids	0.7 g

Perky Piña Colada

Pretend you're on a tropical beach sipping your scrumptious smoothie. Give it a party flair with a skewer of an orange wedge and a ripe strawberry.

Nutrisip: This festive smoothie can also be a terrific healing smoothie. Pineapple contains the enzyme bromelain, which is helpful for fighting inflammation, including sore throats. Omit the dates if you are using the shake for healing, since they contain a lot of date sugar; too much sugar depresses the immune system.

1/2 cup plain soy milk or milk of choice
1 1/2 cups fresh pineapple, peeled and diced
1/3 cup lightly packed grated coconut
1 teaspoon pure vanilla extract
1/2 teaspoon ascorbic acid (vitamin C powder), optional
2 large soft dates, chopped, soaked in a little water first if hard
1 banana, peeled and cut into chunks
6 ice cubes
Garnish: orange slice skewered with a ripe strawberry

Pour the milk into a blender and add the pineapple, coconut, vanilla, ascorbic acid as desired, dates, banana, and ice. Blend on high speed until smooth and serve immediately.

Caribbean Coconut Creme

Total Weight:	16.4 oz.	Serving Size:	8.2 oz.

Serves 2

Basic Components

Calories	174.7
Calories from fat	93.6
Protein	6.1 g
Carbohydrates	15.7 g
Dietary fiber	3.8 g
Sugar—total	10.5 g
Fat—total	10.4 g
Saturated fat	6.8 g
Monounsaturated fat	0.9 g
Polyunsaturated fat	1.7 g

Vitamins

A—beta-carotene	3.7 mcg
Vitamin B6	0.1 mg
Vitamin C	0.7 mg
Vitamin E	0.5 IU
Folate	8.2 mcg

Minerals

Calcium	32.7 mg
Iron	1.6 mg
Magnesium	44.1 mg
Potassium	372.3 mg
Selenium	3.2 mcg
Sodium	17.6 mg
Zinc	0.8 mg

Other Fats

Omega-3 fatty acids	0.1 g
Omega-6 fatty acids	0.5 g

Caribbean Coconut Creme

Coconut gives this smoothie an exotic touch. Sit back, sip away, and pretend you feel those warm, soft island breezes.

Nutrisip: Coconut is a good source of copper, magnesium, and folic acid. Folic acid is involved with vitamin B12 in the synthesis of protein and is important for healthy skin. It is also in great demand during times of stress and pregnancy.

1/2 cup plain soy milk or milk of choice
5 ounces soft silken tofu
1/3 cup grated coconut, lightly packed
3 medium dates, chopped, soaked in a little water first if hard
1 teaspoon pure vanilla extract
6 ice cubes

Pour the milk into a blender and add the tofu, coconut, dates, vanilla, and ice. Blend on high speed until smooth and serve immediately.

Raspberry Ripple

Total Weight:	17.4 oz.	Serving Size:	8.7 oz.

Serves 2

Basic Components

Calories	113.2	Vitamin E	0.7 IU
Calories from fat	5.7	Folate	27.8 mcg
Protein	1.2 g	MINERALS	
Carbohydrates	28.1 g	Calcium	18.7 mg
Dietary fiber	5.6 g	Iron	0.6 mg
Sugar—total	20.9 g	Magnesium	28.9 mg
Fat—total	0.6 g	Potassium	409.5 mg
Saturated fat	0.1 g	Selenium	1.0 mcg
Monounsaturated fat	0.1 g	Sodium	8.3 mg
Polyunsaturated fat	0.3 g	Zinc	0.4 mg
VITAMINS		OTHER FATS	
A—beta-carotene	56.1 mcg	Omega-3 fatty acids	0.1 g
Vitamin B6	0.4 mg	Omega-6 fatty acids	0.2 g
Vitamin C	20.8 mg		

Raspberry Ripple

Garnish with a sprig of mint and you're ready for a poolside party.

Nutrisip: Raspberries are a rich source of anthocyanidins and proanthocyanidins, phytonutrients that support the structure of collagen, which is the major protein structure of skin and bones.

6 frozen Red Zinger tea ice cubes
1/2 cup apple juice (1 apple, juiced)
1 cup fresh or frozen raspberries, rinsed if fresh
1 frozen banana, cut into chunks
6 fresh mint leaves, rinsed
Garnish: sprig of mint (optional)

Steep one Red Zinger tea bag in a cup of hot water for about 20 minutes, or until the tea is strong and flavorful. Pour the tea into six ice cube tray squares and freeze until solid. Pour the apple juice into a blender and add the raspberries, banana, mint, and Red Zinger ice cubes. Blend on high speed until smooth and serve immediately.

Three-Berry Blast

Total Weight:	20.0 oz.	Serving Size:	10.0 oz.

Serves 2

Basic Components

Calories	167.3
Calories from fat	25.7
Protein	6.3 g
Carbohydrates	32.5 g
Dietary fiber	7.2 g
Sugar—total	23.7 g
Fat—total	2.9 g
Saturated fat	0.9 g
Monounsaturated fat	0.5 g
Polyunsaturated fat	0.8 g
Vitamins	
A—beta-carotene	79.3 mcg
Vitamin B6	0.5 mg
Vitamin C	25.8 mg
Vitamin E	1.4 IU
Folate	41.6 mcg
Minerals	
Calcium	138.3 mg
Iron	1.0 mg
Magnesium	54.0 mg
Potassium	612.8 mg
Selenium	4.1 mcg
Sodium	53.1 mg
Zinc	1.1 mg
Other Fats	
Omega-3 fatty acids	0.2 g
Omega-6 fatty acids	0.7 g

Three-Berry Blast

The berries make a darkly rich, colorful drink, and the yogurt makes it creamy. Turn this smoothie into a party special with orange-slice garnishes.

Nutrisip: Berries are a source of catechins, phytonutrients that are shown to support the immune system and help lower cholesterol.

1/2 cup plain soy milk or milk of choice
1/2 cup plain low-fat yogurt
1/2 cup fresh or frozen blueberries, rinsed if fresh
1/2 cup fresh or frozen raspberries, rinsed if fresh
1/2 cup fresh or frozen blackberries, rinsed if fresh
1 frozen banana, cut in chunks
Garnish: two orange slices (optional)

Pour the milk into a blender and add the yogurt, berries, and banana. Blend on high speed until smooth. Garnish with the orange slices as desired and serve immediately.

Tropical Cool-Me-Down

Total Weight: 13.3 oz. Serving Size: 13.3 oz.

Serves 1

Basic Components

Calories	247.1
Calories from fat	131.5
Protein	7.1 g
Carbohydrates	24.1 g
Dietary fiber	8.4 g
Sugar—total	11.6 g
Fat—total	14.6 g
Saturated fat	10.1 g
Monounsaturated fat	1.1 g
Polyunsaturated fat	1.7 g
Vitamins	
A—beta-carotene	83.1 mcg
Vitamin B6	0.1 mg
Vitamin C	99.1 mg
Vitamin E	2.9 IU
Folate	70.0 mcg
Minerals	
Calcium	53.3 mg
Iron	2.0 mg
Magnesium	61.2 mg
Potassium	771.8 mg
Selenium	6.6 mcg
Sodium	33.3 mg
Zinc	0.9 mg
Other Fats	
Omega-3 fatty acids	0.2 g
Omega-6 fatty acids	1.5 g

Tropical Cool-Me-Down

Tastes like a luscious tropical dessert! Garnish with a slice of lime for special occasions.

Nutrisip: Limonoids are phytonutrients found in citrus fruit. They have been studied for their cancer-fighting properties.

1 small papaya, peeled, seeded, and cut into chunks (about 1 1/2 cups)
3/4 cup plain soy milk or milk of choice
1/4 cup grated coconut, lightly packed
1 1/2 teaspoons freshly grated lime peel, preferably organic
1 teaspoon pure vanilla extract
Garnish: lime slice (optional)

Place the papaya chunks in a freezer bag and freeze them until solid. Pour the milk into a blender and add the papaya, coconut, lime peel, and vanilla. Blend on high speed until smooth, garnish with lime slice as desired, and serve immediately.

Strawberry Coconut Creme

Total Weight:	21.6 oz.	Serving Size:	10.8 oz.

Serves 2

Basic Components			
Calories	197.2	Vitamin E	0.5 IU
Calories from fat	93.6	Folate	8.2 mcg
Protein	6.6 g	**Minerals**	
Carbohydrates	21.7 g	Calcium	42.7 mg
Dietary fiber	5.8 g	Iron	2.0 mg
Sugar—total	14.5 g	Magnesium	44.1 mg
Fat—total	10.4 g	Potassium	507.3 mg
Saturated fat	6.9 g	Selenium	3.2 mcg
Monounsaturated fat	0.9 g	Sodium	17.6 mg
Polyunsaturated fat	1.7 g	Zinc	0.8 mg
Vitamins		**Other Fats**	
A—beta-carotene	3.7 mcg	Omega-3 fatty acids	0.1 g
Vitamin B6	0.1 mg	Omega-6 fatty acids	0.5 g
Vitamin C	48.7 mg		

Strawberry Coconut Creme

This smoothie tastes like a summer dessert, and it's actually good for you.

Nutrisip: One interesting study showed that strawberries and spinach had the highest antioxidant activity of 40 popular fruits and vegetables.

1/2 cup plain soy milk or milk of choice
5 ounces soft silken tofu
1/3 cup grated coconut, lightly packed
1 teaspoon pure vanilla extract
8 fresh or frozen strawberries, washed, caps removed, if fresh
3 medium dates, chopped, soaked in a little water first if hard
6 ice cubes

Pour the milk into a blender and add the tofu, coconut, vanilla, strawberries, dates, and ice cubes. Blend on high speed until smooth. Serve immediately.

Rosy Pineapple Punch

Total Weight:	21.4 oz.	Serving Size:	10.7 oz.

Serves 2

Basic Components

Calories	329.6	Vitamin E	11.4 IU
Calories from fat	167.0	Folate	39.4 mcg
Protein	8.6 g	MINERALS	
Carbohydrates	33.7 g	Calcium	108.0 mg
Dietary fiber	8.0 g	Iron	1.9 mg
Sugar—total	23.8 g	Magnesium	133.3 mg
Fat—total	18.6 g	Potassium	648.0 mg
Saturated fat	0.1 g	Selenium	1.2 mcg
Monounsaturated fat	0.1 g	Sodium	3.3 mg
Polyunsaturated fat	0.2 g	Zinc	1.4 mg
VITAMINS		OTHER FATS	
A—beta-carotene	41.8 mcg	Omega-3 fatty acids	0.1 g
Vitamin B6	0.4 mg	Omega-6 fatty acids	0.1 g
Vitamin C	82.4 mg		

Rosy Pineapple Punch

Refreshing on a warm day, this yummy smoothie sports a burst of almond flavor.

Nutrisip: Strawberries are a source of ellagic acid, a superphytonutrient with cancer-fighting effects.

1 cup pineapple juice (1/2 pineapple with core, peeled and juiced)
1 cup fresh or frozen strawberries, washed, caps removed if fresh (8–10 strawberries)
1/2 cup raw almonds
1/4 teaspoon pure almond extract
1 banana, peeled, cut in chunks
6 ice cubes

Pour the pineapple juice into a blender and add the strawberries, almonds, almond extract, banana, and ice. Blend on high speed until smooth and serve immediately.

Berry Smoothie

Total Weight: 15.6 oz. Serving Size: 15.6 oz.

Serves 1

BASIC COMPONENTS

Calories	175.2
Calories from fat	17.8
Protein	6.7 g
Carbohydrates	35.0 g
Dietary fiber	6.4 g
Sugar—total	27.5 g
Fat—total	2.0 g
Saturated fat	1.2 g
Monounsaturated fat	0.5 g
Polyunsaturated fat	0.1 g
VITAMINS	
A—beta-carotene	50.2 mcg
Vitamin B6	0.1 mg
Vitamin C	10.9 mg
Vitamin E	0.2 IU
Folate	23.8 mcg
MINERALS	
Calcium	229.8 mg
Iron	0.6 mg
Magnesium	26.2 mg
Potassium	506.5 mg
Selenium	4.3 mcg
Sodium	96.8 mg
Zinc	1.2 mg
OTHER FATS	
Omega-3 fatty acids	0.0 g
Omega-6 fatty acids	0.1 g

Berry Smoothie

Special for the holidays; terrific flavor all year. Dress up this smoothie with a strawberry or mint leaf garnish for a special presentation.

Nutrisip: Cranberries are rich in vitamin C, anthocyanidins, and proanthocyanidins, nutrients that support healthy bones and connective tissue.

1/2 cup apple juice (1 Red Delicious or other sweet apple, washed and juiced)
1/2 cup plain low-fat yogurt
1/4 cup fresh or frozen cranberries, rinsed if fresh
1 small piece fresh beet (for color)
6 ice cubes
Garnish: sprig of mint or strawberry (optional)

Pour the apple juice into a blender and add the yogurt, cranberries, beet, and ice. Blend on high speed until smooth. Garnish with mint or strawberry as desired and serve immediately.

Just Desserts

When you're hungry for something sweet, you can healthfully satisfy that sweet tooth with the frozen dessert recipes in this book, which have no refined sugar. Sugar puts a demand on the body to supply extra nutrients, such as chromium, for metabolism. Also, sugar will beat out nutrients like vitamin C and beta-carotene for entry into white blood cells. You then run the risk of compromising your immune system. But frozen smoothies, which I've turned into sorbets, sherbets, and ices, are made with fresh fruit, other natural ingredients, and a little honey. They are infinitely better for you than commercial ice cream and other frozen desserts.

Most of the fruit smoothie recipes outside this chapter can be made into frozen desserts by adding to the recipe 1 tablespoon to 1/4 cup honey. Next, blend on high speed until smooth, pour into a freezer bag or bowl with cover, and freeze until solid. When ready, remove the mixture from the freezer bag/bowl and place it on a cutting board. Chop with a knife into one- to two-inch chunks and put them in a food processor; blend until smooth. Spoon the mixture into dessert cups and serve immediately or return to the freezer, covered, until ready to serve. Or follow the simple instructions for any recipe in this chapter and make yourself a yummy dessert like Very Berry Sorbet (page 315) or Peppermint Party Ice (page 313).

I've dedicated this chapter to the homeless children of America—children who may rarely get dessert, who may not regularly get dinner, and who have no home to call their own. The average age of a homeless person in the United States is nine years old. At the time of this writing, the Colorado Coalition for the Homeless, to which I often donate, is sponsoring a campaign in conjunction with many Denver restaurants called Just Desserts; the proceeds will go toward helping homeless children. I've borrowed their campaign slogan as my chapter title. I'm donating a portion of my royalties from this book to the Coalition's campaign for homeless children. I invite you to donate, too. Donations can be sent to the Colorado Coalition for Homeless Children, 2100 Broadway, Denver, CO 80205. Or you may wish to donate to such a coalition in your state.

Green Tea Pear Sorbet

Total Weight: 19.8 oz. Serving Size: 9.9 oz.

Serves 2

Basic Components

Calories	129.3
Calories from fat	4.1
Protein	1.0 g
Carbohydrates	32.6 g
Dietary fiber	2.1 g
Sugar—total	28.3 g
Fat—total	0.5 g
Saturated fat	0.0 g
Monounsaturated fat	0.1 g
Polyunsaturated fat	0.1 g
Vitamins	
A—beta-carotene	17.1 mcg
Vitamin B6	0.1 mg
Vitamin C	50.3 mg
Vitamin E	0.7 IU
Folate	18.9 mcg
Minerals	
Calcium	20.9 mg
Iron	0.5 mg
Magnesium	20.0 mg
Potassium	309.3 mg
Selenium	1.0 mcg
Sodium	1.7 mg
Zinc	0.2 mg
Other Fats	
Omega-3 fatty acids	0.0 g
Omega-6 fatty acids	0.1 g

Green Tea Pear Sorbet

This frozen dessert reminds me of a number of palate-cleansing sorbets I've tasted in fine restaurants. Now, you can make your restaurant-quality sorbet at home.

Nutrisip: Green tea has been shown in clinical studies to reduce cholesterol and triglycerides and increase the good HDL cholesterol. Combine that with the heart-healthy properties of grapes, and you have a good-for-your-heart dessert.

6 green tea ice cubes
1 cup white grape juice (2 cups green grapes, juiced)
1 ripe medium pear, washed, stem removed, and cut into chunks
1 tablespoon honey

Steep one bag of green tea in a cup of hot water for about 20 minutes, or until the tea is strong and flavorful. Pour the tea into six ice cube tray squares and freeze. Pour the grape juice into a blender and add the pear, honey, and green tea ice cubes. Blend on high speed until the mixture is smooth, pour it into a freezer bag, and freeze. Remove the frozen mixture from the freezer bag and place it on a cutting board. Chop with a knife into one- to two-inch chunks, place the frozen chunks in a food processor, and blend until smooth. You may need to stop the food processor occasionally and scrape the sides with a rubber spatula. Spoon into dessert cups and serve immediately or cover the cups and return to the freezer until ready to serve.

Cantaloupe Mint Sorbet

Total Weight: 12.8 oz. Serving Size: 3.2 oz.

Serves 4

BASIC COMPONENTS

Calories	88.7
Calories from fat	1.8
Protein	0.7 g
Carbohydrates	23.3 g
Dietary fiber	0.6 g
Sugar—total	21.8 g
Fat—total	0.2 g
Saturated fat	0.1 g
Monounsaturated fat	0.0 g
Polyunsaturated fat	0.1 g
VITAMINS	
A—beta-carotene	1329.9 mcg
Vitamin B6	0.1 mg
Vitamin C	29.3 mg
Vitamin E	0.2 IU
Folate	12.4 mcg
MINERALS	
Calcium	9.4 mg
Iron	0.2 mg
Magnesium	8.2 mg
Potassium	225.4 mg
Selenium	0.5 mcg
Sodium	7.1 mg
Zinc	0.2 mg
OTHER FATS	
Omega-3 fatty acids	0.0 g
Omega-6 fatty acids	0.0 g

Cantaloupe Mint Sorbet

Make this dessert when you want to really impress someone, but you don't have the time to work at it. It has a beautiful pastel peach color with little flecks of mint—like something you'd discover in a great restaurant. You can make this dessert in five minutes, but it will look and taste as if you've slaved in the kitchen for hours.

Nutrisip: Cantaloupe is a good source of beta-carotene, vitamin C, and potassium, yet low in calories, making this a guilt-free dessert.

1/2 cantaloupe, peeled, seeds removed
16 fresh mint leaves, rinsed
1/4 cup honey or to taste

Cut the cantaloupe into approximately 1-inch chunks and freeze them in a freezer bag until solid. Put the frozen cantaloupe chunks in a food processor and add the mint and honey. Blend until smooth. You may need to stop the food processor occasionally and scrape the sides with a rubber spatula. Spoon the mixture into dessert cups and serve immediately or cover the cups and return to the freezer until ready to serve.

Anise Ice

Total Weight:	18.6 oz.	Serving Size:	6.2 oz.

Serves 3

Basic Components		Vitamin E	0.4 IU
Calories	122.9	Folate	8.7 mcg
Calories from fat	2.4	Minerals	
Protein	0.5 g	Calcium	16.8 mg
Carbohydrates	31.5 g	Iron	0.4 mg
Dietary fiber	2.3 g	Magnesium	7.9 mg
Sugar—total	26.4 g	Potassium	171.3 mg
Fat—total	0.3 g	Selenium	1.0 mcg
Saturated fat	0.0 g	Sodium	10.5 mg
Monounsaturated fat	0.1 g	Zinc	0.2 mg
Polyunsaturated fat	0.1 g	Other Fats	
Vitamins		Omega-3 fatty acids	0.0 g
A—beta-carotene	25.5 mcg	Omega-6 fatty acids	0.1 g
Vitamin B6	0.0 mg		
Vitamin C	4.6 mg		

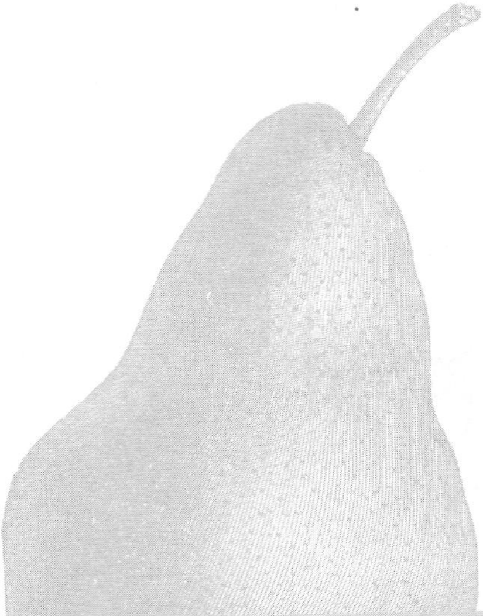

Anise Ice

After a rich gourmet meal, this light dessert will help digestion and refresh the palate. This recipe got the most votes from my taste testers as the best dessert.

Nutrisip: Anise is an ancient remedy that eases indigestion, as do mint and fennel.

1/2 cup fresh fennel juice (3–4 stalks fennel with leaves)
1/2 cup unsweetened applesauce
1/2 teaspoon pure anise extract
3 tablespoons honey
6 mint leaves, rinsed
1 ripe pear, washed, stem removed, and cut into chunks

Pour the fennel juice into a blender and add the applesauce, anise, honey, mint, and pear. Blend on high speed until smooth and pour the mixture into a freezer bag. When completely frozen, remove the mixture from the freezer bag and place it on a cutting board. Chop it with a knife into one- to two-inch chunks and put the chunks in a food processor. Blend until smooth. You may need to stop the food processor occasionally and scrape the sides with a rubber spatula. Spoon the mixture into dessert cups and serve immediately or cover the cups and return to the freezer until ready to serve.

Peppermint Party Ice

Total Weight: 19.2 oz. Serving Size: 9.6 oz.

Serves 2

Basic Components

Calories	178.8
Calories from fat	5.1
Protein	1.1 g
Carbohydrates	45.8 g
Dietary fiber	3.4 g
Sugar—total	39.3 g
Fat—total	0.6 g
Saturated fat	0.0 g
Monounsaturated fat	0.1 g
Polyunsaturated fat	0.2 g

Vitamins

A—beta-carotene	54.6 mcg
Vitamin B6	0.1 mg
Vitamin C	55.4 mg
Vitamin E	1.3 IU
Folate	17.3 mcg

Minerals

Calcium	27.4 mg
Iron	0.7 mg
Magnesium	25.0 mg
Potassium	349.5 mg
Selenium	1.3 mcg
Sodium	4.2 mg
Zinc	0.3 mg

Other Fats

Omega-3 fatty acids	0.0 g
Omega-6 fatty acids	0.2 g

Peppermint Party Ice

This is a light, refreshing dessert after a heavy meal or a hot spicy one.

Nutrisip: Peppermint contains an oil, azulene, that is said to have anti-inflammatory and ulcer-healing effects. Mint is also known to be good for digestion.

6 peppermint herbal tea ice cubes
1/2 cup white grape juice (1 cup green grapes picked from large stems and juiced)
1 ripe pear, stem removed and cut into chunks
1 kiwifruit, peeled and cut into chunks
2–3 tablespoons honey
1/8 teaspoon pure peppermint extract

Steep one peppermint herbal tea bag in a cup of hot water for about 20 minutes, or until the tea is strong and flavorful. Pour the tea into six ice cube tray squares and freeze. Pour the grape juice into a blender and add the pear, kiwi, honey, peppermint extract, and peppermint tea ice cubes. Blend on high speed until smooth. Pour the mixture into a freezer bag, and when it is completely frozen, remove the mixture from the freezer and place on a cutting board. Chop the mixture with a knife into one- to two-inch chunks and put the chunks in a food processor. Blend until smooth. You may need to stop the food processor occasionally and scrape the sides with a rubber spatula. Spoon the mixture into dessert cups and serve immediately or cover the cups and return to the freezer until ready to serve.

Very Berry Sorbet

Total Weight:	21.6 oz.	Serving Size:	10.8 oz.

Serves 2

Basic Components			
Calories	231.8	Vitamin E	1.4 IU
Calories from fat	25.7	Folate	42.0 mcg
Protein	6.4 g	**Minerals**	
Carbohydrates	50.0 g	Calcium	139.6 mg
Dietary fiber	7.2 g	Iron	1.1 mg
Sugar—total	40.2 g	Magnesium	54.4 mg
Fat—total	2.9 g	Potassium	623.8 mg
Saturated fat	0.9 g	Selenium	4.3 mcg
Monounsaturated fat	0.5 g	Sodium	54.0 mg
Polyunsaturated fat	0.8 g	Zinc	1.1 mg
Vitamins		**Other Fats**	
A—beta-carotene	79.3 mcg	Omega-3 fatty acids	0.2 g
Vitamin B6	0.5 mg	Omega-6 fatty acids	0.7 g
Vitamin C	25.9 mg		

Very Berry Sorbet

A pretty bright, berry-red dessert.

Nutrisip: Blackberries are a good fruit source of folic acid, which functions with vitamin B12 in many body processes. Though folic acid occurs widely in plant foods, it is one of the most common vitamin deficiencies in the world.

1/2 cup plain soy milk or milk of choice
1/2 cup plain low-fat yogurt
1/2 cup fresh or frozen blueberries, rinsed if fresh
1/2 cup fresh or frozen raspberries, rinsed if fresh
1/2 cup fresh or frozen blackberries, rinsed if fresh
2 tablespoons honey
1 banana, peeled and cut in chunks

Pour the milk into a blender and add the yogurt, berries, honey, and banana. Blend on high speed until smooth. Pour the mixture into a freezer bag and freeze. When it is completely frozen, remove the mixture from the bag and place it on a cutting board. Chop it with a knife into one- to two-inch chunks and put them in a food processor. Blend until smooth. You may need to stop the food processor occasionally and scrape the sides with a rubber spatula. Spoon mixture into dessert cups and serve immediately or return to the freezer, covered, until ready to serve.

Pineapple Delight

Total Weight:	16.4 oz.	Serving Size:	8.2 oz.

Serves 2

BASIC COMPONENTS			
Calories	134.1	Vitamin E	1.0 IU
Calories from fat	0.7	Folate	3.7 mcg
Protein	0.7 g	MINERALS	
Carbohydrates	34.5 g	Calcium	6.8 mg
Dietary fiber	1.7 g	Iron	0.2 mg
Sugar—total	30.1 g	Magnesium	7.0 mg
Fat—total	0.1 g	Potassium	261.7 mg
Saturated fat	0.0 g	Selenium	0.5 mcg
Monounsaturated fat	0.0 g	Sodium	4.0 mg
Polyunsaturated fat	0.0 g	Zinc	0.2 mg
VITAMINS		OTHER FATS	
A—beta-carotene	249.1 mcg	Omega-3 fatty acids	0.0 g
Vitamin B6	0.0 mg	Omega-6 fatty acids	0.0 g
Vitamin C	20.7 mg		

Pineapple Delight

This is a yummy pineapple sorbet.

Nutrisip: Pineapple is rich in the enzyme bromelain, which helps such health conditions as angina, arthritis, indigestion, and sports injuries.

6 chamomile herbal tea ice cubes
1/2 cup pineapple juice (about 1/4 pineapple, peeled and juiced; core can be juiced)
1 cup fresh or frozen peaches, sliced; peeled if fresh
2 tablespoons honey

Steep one chamomile herbal tea bag in a cup of hot water for about 20 minutes or until the tea is strong and flavorful. Pour the tea into six ice cube tray squares and freeze. Pour the pineapple juice into a blender and add the peaches, honey, and chamomile tea ice cubes. Blend on high speed until smooth. Pour the mixture into a freezer bag and freeze until solid. When it is completely frozen, remove it from the freezer and place it on a cutting board. Chop the mixture with a knife into one- to two-inch chunks and put the chunks in a food processor. Blend until smooth. Spoon the mixture into dessert cups and serve immediately or return to the freezer, covered, until ready to serve. If it is stored more than two or three days, you may need to put the mixture in the food processor again and blend before serving.

Just Peachy Creme Sorbet

Total Weight:	16.4 oz.	Serving Size:	8.2 oz.

Serves 2

Basic Components

Calories	145.0
Calories from fat	9.3
Protein	3.9 g
Carbohydrates	31.4 g
Dietary fiber	1.7 g
Sugar—total	28.4 g
Fat—total	1.0 g
Saturated fat	0.6 g
Monounsaturated fat	0.3 g
Polyunsaturated fat	0.1 g
Vitamins	
A—beta-carotene	225.8 mcg
Vitamin B6	0.1 mg
Vitamin C	6.2 mg
Vitamin E	0.9 IU
Folate	10.6 mcg
Minerals	
Calcium	118.7 mg
Iron	0.3 mg
Magnesium	17.7 mg
Potassium	327.4 mg
Selenium	2.5 mcg
Sodium	44.5 mg
Zinc	0.7 mg
Other Fats	
Omega-3 fatty acids	0.0 g
Omega-6 fatty acids	0.1 g

Just Peachy Creme Sorbet

A beautiful dessert. Top with fresh mint leaves for a spectacular presentation.

Nutrisip: Peaches are low in calories and provide potassium, carotenes, and flavonoids.

6 peach herbal tea ice cubes
1/2 cup plain low-fat yogurt
2 tablespoons honey
1 teaspoon pure vanilla extract
1 cup fresh peaches, peeled, pitted, and chopped (about 1 peach; frozen peaches can be substituted)
Garnish: fresh mint leaves (optional)

Steep one peach herbal tea bag in a cup of hot water for about 20 minutes or until the tea is strong and flavorful. Pour the tea into six ice cube tray squares and freeze. Combine the yogurt in a blender with the honey, vanilla, peaches, and peach ice cubes. Blend on high speed until smooth. Pour the mixture into a freezer bag and freeze until solid. Remove it from the bag and place on a cutting board. Chop the mixture with a knife into one- to two-inch chunks and put the chunks in a food processor. Blend until smooth. You may need to stop the food processor occasionally and scrape the sides with a rubber spatula. Spoon the mixture into dessert cups and serve immediately or return to the freezer, covered, until ready to serve. If it is stored more than two or three days, you may need to put the mixture in the food processor again and blend before serving.

Lemon Dream Milk Shake

Total Weight: 11.8 oz. Serving Size: 11.8 oz.

Serves 1

Basic Components

Calories	236.4
Calories from fat	23.9
Protein	13.1 g
Carbohydrates	42.0 g
Dietary fiber	2.0 g
Sugar—total	38.8 g
Fat—total	2.7 g
Saturated fat	0.5 g
Monounsaturated fat	0.5 g
Polyunsaturated fat	1.0 g
Vitamins	
A—beta-carotene	2.7 mcg
Vitamin B6	0.2 mg
Vitamin C	12.4 mg
Vitamin E	0.1 IU
Folate	24.7 mcg
Minerals	
Calcium	344.5 mg
Iron	0.9 mg
Magnesium	56.7 mg
Potassium	624.9 mg
Selenium	1.6 mcg
Sodium	143.7 mg
Zinc	1.9 mg
Other Fats	
Omega-3 fatty acids	0.1 g
Omega-6 fatty acids	0.9 g

Lemon Dream Milk Shake

Bet you've never dreamed a lemon shake could taste this good.

Nutrisip: Lemons contain a phytonutrient known as limonene, which is helpful in dissolving gallstones and has also demonstrated some anti-cancer effects.

1/2 cup plain soy milk or milk of choice
*1 cup frozen vanilla Rice Dream**
1 tablespoon fresh lemon juice, lemon peeled if using a juice machine
1/2 teaspoon freshly grated lemon peel, preferably organic

Pour the milk into a blender and add the frozen Rice Dream, lemon juice, and lemon peel. Blend on high speed until smooth and serve immediately. For a different version add 1/2 cup fresh (rinsed) or frozen blueberries for a blueberry-lemon milk shake.

**Rice Dream frozen desserts are made of rice cream that is naturally sweetened with brown rice syrup and taste like ice cream. They can be found at most health food stores.*

Afterword

If you've heard it once, you've heard it hundreds of times: "Eat your vegetables!" And I would add, "Eat your fruit, too." You know you should. But most of us know we don't eat enough of either. Countless scientific studies have proved that a diet rich in vegetables and fruits can improve your health, prevent disease, boost your energy levels, and enhance your overall well-being. But you have a busy life, and all that slicing and dicing of fruits and vegetables takes a lot of time. What to do?

Smoothies offer an answer to your nutritional needs and an easy fit for your busy lifestyle. Just combine fresh fruits, vegetables, juice, soy milk or tofu, and ice in your blender and you have a vitamin-rich drink that tastes good. Really good! It's something the whole family will love and so easy to make even the kids can combine their favorite ingredients. And you can have the assurance that everyone in the family is getting closer to their vegetable and fruit servings each day.

I hope you enjoy my smoothie recipes. Most of all, I wish you the best of health—one of the most precious gifts you'll ever have.

Index

About the Author

Known as a leading expert on nutrition, Cherie Calbom has earned a master of science degree in nutrition from Bastyr University. She frequently appears on QVC and speaks nationwide on the benefits of juicing and healthy living. She has written eight previous books. Cherie lives with her husband, John, in Evergreen, Colorado.